Is Your Self-Worth Pseudo
A Guide to Honesty with S

Is Your Self-Worth Pseudo or Sincere?
A Guide to Honesty with Self

Copyright 2017 by Yah-I Ausar Tafari Amen

Published by Yah-I Ausar Tafari Amen
www.lovebeingapart.com

Cover Design by Constant Elevation

Edited by Abena Bediako, Ma'at em Maakheru Amen

Contact the Author
yahi@lovebeingapart.com
Info@veganflavacafe.com
www.lovebeingapart.com

Acknowledgements

The All in all

I give thanks for my ancestors and the ancestors who have taught and influenced me accordingly including, but emphatically not limited to: my father, Sinclair A. Towe Sr., my cultural, spiritual and artistic fathers and teachers, Baba Kwame Ishangi and Baba Charles R. Davis 'Baba Chuck'.

I give thanks my wife, who has contributed so much to my spiritual growth, development, and execution. I give thanks for our partnerships and her inspiration having already written two books.

I give thanks for my children, with special mention to my oldest daughter for her input.

I give thanks for my mother who has been relentless in supporting and encouraging me every step of the way. I know exactly why I chose her.

I give thanks for family, siblings, aunts, uncles, cousins and In-Laws who have been supportive in so many ways.

I give thanks for my closest of friends who I have remained in constant contact with over the decades and have helped me tremendously: I-Ras, Troy, Glenn, Antar, Osun Woyuolo Efunlayo (Sister Pearl), Khepera and Auset, Ra Herakthy, Divine, Abena, Taynov, Heru Khuti, Het Heru.

I give thanks for my African American Dance Ensemble family and the community of Elders and others in the dance and drum community who have taught and supported me. Special acknowledgement to Baba Ngoma, Mama Norma and Mama E'Vonne.

I give thanks for my Vegan Flava Café (Triangle) community, Anita Woodley, Knotti by Nature, Taji's Hair Salon, Locks, Nails and More, Simply Yours, Ms Cee, Bro Stephen, Elder Yousef, Brother Rashid El, Bro Al, Sister BriAnkhah, Cuz Michael Price, St Sya Acadamy, Blue Dogwood Market, The Beat Making Lab, Shabutaso, Nu Community Development Center, Marc Lee and Hayti Family, Spirit House, Mocha Moms friends, Nubian Natural Hair Gallery, Motherland Vibrations, BlacKnight Durham Studios, Durham Co-op Market, Black Genius, Black August, Peach Cobbler Yoga, Beautiful By Design, Himidi Productions, Water for Life Wellness Center, Jasmaya

Publishing, The Life Society, Eric Kelly, Baba Egungun, our regular customers, staff, past and present and other dear friends.

I give thanks for WRFG 89.3 Atlanta family, Sister Kai Aiyetoro, Brother Akenaton, Brother Wanique, Khemi Tehuti Shabazz. Aba Shaka, Ras Kofi, Princess of the Posse, Panther Power Hour crew. WURD 900am Philadelphia, Sarah Lomax Reese, Cody Anderson, and Bill Anderson.

I give thanks for IMG Consulting and the fantastic and thorough assistance and services of Harold Causby and Vernita Sherman

I give thanks for all of the folks I am linked to who have displayed only love and support no matter how long it has been since we last connected.

Is Your Self-Worth Pseudo or Sincere?
A Guide to Honesty with Self

Introduction

Everything in life has some degree of value we place on it. Our life journey includes identifying and assessing that value, which begins, most importantly, with the self. What is it worth to 'you' for 'me' to be here in your presence? That is a question that may or may not actually be asked outright but is covertly contemplated. With this value and worth concept in mind, I thought about the ultimate displays and results of de-valuing life. Those results are accounted for in suicide and homicide rates, though not exclusively.

The suicide rates double that of homicides in the US and around the world, for the most part. When something lacks value, it is easily discarded. I had no idea that more people took their own life, more so, than having it taken from them. As I worked on this book I saw just how pertinent it was to see and celebrate that value we identify as self-worth.

The purpose of this book is to define and examine the irrefutable benefits of developing and maintaining a strong and sincere sense of self-worth, while, simultaneously dismantling the infiltration of a trivial, distracting, destructive and often fatal pseudo self-worth. This book has helped me to realize that with every waking moment we spend with our respective selves, we communicate and make decisions accordingly. I have already regarded, in life, the concept that there is a thin line between needing or not needing to care about what someone thinks of you. I challenge you, in this book, to operate out of a place of knowing which side of the line you fall on.

Every decision to say, do, not say or not do something has an opportunity to add value to your self-worth. Together we will journey through the beginnings of my interpretation of self-worth actualization as it is introduced to us in childhood and is assessed right into and through adulthood and elderhood. I will use a working and practical definition of both concepts along with some supportive verbiage that will make sense to even a 5-year-old.

I do wish to make a distinction between self-worth and self-esteem just to iterate the importance of this self-worth focus. I googled these terms and they were defined as follows:

Self-worth is the opinion you have about yourself and the value you place on yourself, the sense of one's own value or worth as a person.

In sociology and psychology, self-esteem reflects a person's overall subjective emotional evaluation of his or her own worth. It is a judgment of oneself as well as an attitude toward the self. Self-esteem means 'feeling good about ourselves'.

If your self-esteem is high, based on a false or pseudo sense of worth, that fabricated realization can and will lead to resentment of self and seemingly cause a frantic scramble for peace, balance, and acceptance of whom you really are. You would have lived your life, up to whatever point, as a lie and may not recover quickly enough to get to a sincere place of self-worth. What this ultimately says is you can feel good about yourself and still lack sincere self-worth.

Another term to add to the reasoning is, Worthy.

Worthy - having or showing the qualities or abilities that merit recognition in a specified way.

We will examine our 'worthiness' when it comes to being in the presence of others and how that plays a role when operating out of a sincere place or a made-up, pseudo place.

By the time you finish this book you will see how everything can be reconciled by looking through the lenses of self-worth. The President of the United States of America is one of the poster children of pseudo self-worth. That also goes for anyone you know who does not take feedback well or cannot be wrong about anything. What he shows us is, you can be a billionaire and have sincere self-worth, but still do plenty out of a place of pseudo self-worth.

If you are willing to look, you will you see your reflection of self in everyone. If you have been cheated on you will see self-worth as a component of the relationship violation. Upon reading this book you will see clearly, the fine line between confidence and arrogance within you. With honesty, you will see, reflect upon and change what you do, when, why and how you do it.

You will not think about children, social media, driving, sports, relationships, religion, eating and people in authority the same way once you put to practice this concept of pseudo and sincere self-worth. I suspect you will encourage me to address the many subjects I left out of this book, in the next volume, once you begin to look at the source of your self-worth in life experiences. I will for you, Joyful reading and honest reflecting.

Table of Contents

1. WHAT IS SINCERE SELF-WORTH (SSW) AND PSEUDO SELF-WORTH (PSW)

2. BIRTHING AND BUILDING SELF-WORTH

3. SELF-WORTH AT A MOST CRUCIAL TIME, YOUNG ADULTHOOD

4. REAL-TIME CONTRIBUTION TO SELF-WORTH WITH SOCIAL MEDIA

5. IS YOUR SELF-WORTH DRIVING YOU MAD?

6. SPORTING SELF WORTH

7. THE SELF-WORTH FACTOR IN BULLYING

8. AM I WORTHY TO BE A PART OF THIS RELIGION?

9. IS THIS FOOD WORTHY TO BE INSIDE ME?

10. PSEUDO SELF WORTH MEANS I GET SOME, SINCERE SELF-WORTH MEANS I GIVE IT UP

11. MOVING FORWARD MOST PROGRESSIVELY

Chapter I

What is Sincere Self-Worth (SSW) and Pseudo Self-Worth (PSW)

Sincere Self-Worth (SSW) is when you see and/or add value to yourself. SSW can be obtained, maintained or enhanced by employing this simple concept. You add value to yourself by completing tasks, achieving stated goals, taking certain actions that allow you to feel great about yourself or not reacting to situations that could make for undesirable circumstances. SSW recognizes your skills and talents professionally and creatively. SSW celebrates accomplishments in the categories including but not limited to being; honest, disciplined, patient, non-judgmental, respectful, calm, proactive, focused, i.e., (breathing or meditating), prompt, helpful, efficient, thoughtful, giving, responsible, dedicated, committed, peaceful and joyful.

A key component of SSW is that it does not warrant the recognition of others necessarily. You can and do celebrate you and your achievements in your mind. Your SSW is displayed in all that you do naturally. If you are an athlete, performing or visual artist, others may have applaud you accordingly, but you felt great about yourself and your work long before anyone else experienced it.

In the introduction, I mentioned the degree to which you should care what people think of you. I must expound on my position with this, especially as it pertains to defining sincere and pseudo self-worth. The rule is very simple: If you can dictate and/or make a decision that will impact my grade, my loan, my role on the team, my business venture, my employment, my election, etc., I care about what you think of me and will be intentional in how I present myself. If your regard for me, or lack thereof will have no impact on anything except how I feel about myself, I cannot provide you with that 'power'.

If you are a random person in the street looking at me sideways because of what I am wearing, what my hair looks like, or what my opinion is on the racial biases and injustices in America, your opinion has no bearing or effect on my life. Therefore, I cannot afford to care about what you think of me. There is no value in caring what you think about me.

I had to learn this the hard way. I spent and wasted a lot of time deciding on what to wear or what brand of clothes or sneakers to buy, making certain you recognized the designer. I was late for school in high school 4 out of 5 days a week because of this obsession with what others thought of me. I used to save my designer tags and displayed them just in case someone came over, so they could see all the different 'expensive', 'popular' tags I collected over the years. What I learned was, it did not matter how you regarded me if it was based on what designer I was wearing. I did not become a better person because of the tag stitched on my garments. I do feel better about myself when I am wearing something hand-made like what Marla Hawkins makes. But there again, it has nothing to do with you. It has everything to do with me celebrating supporting someone whom I love and respect. She does quality work and puts her energy into everything she makes, from bags to quilts to clothes.

I have learned and experienced that if everyone were in a state of SSW mostly, the world would be a better place. Everyone would experience an inner peace and sincere sense of joy that would feed all life forms around us, humans, animals, plants and insects alike. SSW is essential to our existence whereas its arch nemesis, Pseudo Self Worth will continue to taunt and haunt the progress of humanity until the end of time.

When we feel great about self, we feel great about our extensions of self, each other. When we are in a great mood, we greet and infect everyone around us with our progressive vibrations. When we sincerely value our respective selves, we do not care about what other people might think about us.

I must now offer a basic, practical definition of Pseudo Self-Worth. PSW value is added to you by way of one's recognition or celebration of something you possess, have done and/or have expressed. PSW value can also be added by an intentionally taking no action in a given situation. The foundation of PSW is that it requires other entities and their standards to be factored into your actions or inaction.

You possess things in hopes that other people take notice and celebrate or relate to you because of those things instead of who you are innate. You do things to be noticed, and with the attention you have drawn in, you have established or increased you PSW. You can get the same level of attention or notoriety by sitting idle while others take some action like refusing to participate in a group effort of some sort.

If someone offers instruction for a group of people you are with, you will be the one to refuse to follow those instructions, when you are operating out of PSW. You might even vocalize your lack of intent to respond to the request to draw more attention to yourself. You will call for attention even people will not see you in a favorable light. If people talked about you after, you left an imprint in their minds and your mission was then complete. You drew attention to yourself and added PSW in the process.

The areas covered in highlighting PSW are pretty much the same as with SSW but the motives and outcomes are drastically different. You responded affirmatively to the instruction given to the group because you take pride in cooperating, being respectful and leading by example.

I am going to talk a lot about me when offering my support for my premise. I do not wish for this self-worth conversation to be about judgment, though it will involve observing the behaviors of others. I look forward to us seeing the reflection of self in others and being honest with self.

For the past 30 years, I have been trying to get ready for the summer by working out such that I will be physically appealing to the masses of women. The personal accomplishment of working out makes for a great opportunity to feel good about me, but it is rooted in PSW. I want to be muscularly appealing so that women will like my body and offer seductive looks, and smiles. I think and wish; maybe some stranger in a revealing bikini will approach me and ask if she can put shea butter on my muscles. I know the fantasy is supposed to include suntan lotion but shea butter is my all-in-one skin treatment.

Watching TV, movies and the seeing my female friends act out lustfully, when they see a muscular body, has certainly contributed to this

desire. I recall switching from boxer briefs to bikini briefs because one of my friends got tremendous attention when he wore his bikini style bathing suit (Speedos) while on a group beach trip, back when I was a teenager.
I have not been successful at fulfilling this 'cock-diesel' beach body goal as of yet. I usually get off to a great start every spring. I get deep into my workouts until I get too busy or lazy or just no longer 'beach body' inspired. Though I clearly recognize how beneficial it is to be stronger, that has not been my leading motivation for working out. My main motivation has been to get looks and attention, which is all about PSW. If I were operating out of a pure SSW space, I would do my daily 40-80 pull-ups, 100 push-ups, sun salutation and 500 jumps with my rope, on the strength of discipline and determination.
I would like to shift my thinking so that I remain consistent because I feel better about myself when I am consistent, disciplined and focused. I know that I am not served in any substantial way by a random woman approaching me and rubbing my chest. It probably makes for less drama seeing as my wife is not too supportive of a random woman feeling on me lustfully either. It was probably ok 30 years ago when I was a hormonal teenager.
This is not to say that I have no discipline or focus, or that I am not consistent in any area

of my life. It is suggesting that I am selective about how I apply my spiritual self to various areas of living and being. I have enough SSW to feel great about myself despite this area of opportunity. This is one of the most significant lessons I wish to get across to the masses. My net-worth is 'in the black' even though I have plenty of deficiencies and opportunities to improve upon, which may be deemed 'in the red'. I am confident that you can relate.

Many of us are disciplined when it comes to our workout but cannot or do not apply the same discipline when it comes to eating, gossiping, drinking alcohol without a designated driver or watching the NFL even though there is a boycott. We can look at patience, commitment, awareness, focus and other areas of personal growth and development the same way.

As a teenager, I was relatively short but had a nice game on the basketball court. At the time I was living in Lefrak City Queens with my mother and staying with my father in East New York and Bushwick, Brooklyn on the weekends. During the week, especially in the summer, I would go to the basketball court alone. The court was 'over the bridge', which was the walkway over the Long Island Expressway.

There, I would enhance my ball handling skills and finesse my shooting techniques for getting the ball into the basket elusively. I would spend hours practicing. I told no one about my efforts and had no need for an audience. Later on that day I would go back out once everyone got home from summer camp and put in to practice what I worked on. I felt even better about myself from earlier in the day because I was able to implement and execute what I worked on such that my street court stock rose in value as well as my SSW.

I was only 5'6" but was very close to dunking because I spent a lot of time at home working on my calf lifts and deep knee bends. Again, I felt great about myself because I had these goals and accomplishments constantly being worked on consistently and effectively. Every day I reflected on how I improved and what I did to contribute to those improvements. I worked with myself and for myself without needing any public recognition for my self-development efforts. My skill set could be observed and recognized based on how I played but I knew, whether I won or lost, how 'nice' I was becoming. I was adding value to myself from the conception of building skills to actually seeing the results. I was well on my way to playing college and professional ball. That was my plan back then.

I am clear that part of being skilled in basketball also included being sweated by dudes and women. My PSW was certainly also a beneficiary of me having game and being picked more often over others to run a full court game. If you play ball, you know how it is to be picked first and the first time around. This goes the same for being picked for any team of any sort. I would not be honest if I did not acknowledge that it 'sucked' to have to sit out the first game and have to call next. I wanted to be known for anything and everything I did well.

While living in Atlanta, my good bredren, I-Ras Levi, invited me to co-host his radio show, Ruff, Rugged and Raw. It was an uncensored Hip Hop and Reggae that aired on WRFG 89.3 on Wednesday Mornings from 3am-6am. Up until this point, I was just a hip-hop connoisseur making cassette tapes off the radio because I did not have the money to buy the records or CDs. That was in 1994. I purchased my first pair of Technique 1200's from a friend and DJ, Justice, of the Famous EarWax Records. I began to build, very rapidly, a hefty record collection.

Justice taught me how to blend records and Talib Shabazz, a fellow radio host and DJ, taught me about song selections and putting together a set. Every Tuesday when I got paid I would spend a certain amount on record purchases at Ear Wax and at the used records section in thrift stores. Every several months I would go home and hit my favorite record stores in Brooklyn and Manhattan, Beat Street and Rock and Soul respectively.

I share this background information because it makes for another SSW building block. I grew up on Hip Hop, R&B and Reggae and loved the weekend, because I could hear new hits and live mixes on 92.3 WKTU, 98.7 WRKS, 89.9 WKCR, 105.9 WNWK and 107.5 WBLS from Red Alert, Chuck Chillout, Mr. Magic, David Levy, Stretch and Bobitto, Special K and Teddy Ted, and Carlos, to name a few.

From a PSW perspective, I looked up to all of those DJs and personalities on the radio growing up and now I had the potential to be one of them. I was going to be 'famous' even though no one could see me. I loved it. I was elated to have the opportunity to bring music to folks over the airwaves the same way it was brought to me. I also loved people recognizing my voice when I was grocery shopping or at some other public place. I built my craft and passion in hopes that the listeners enjoyed the music as much as I enjoyed playing it. My SSW was expanded tremendously during this time. It was nice to hear that people who listened appreciated my selections but it was not necessary as long as I knew I was getting better and better on producing, selecting and mixing accordingly.

For the past 25 years, I have been a performing artist. I first started doing African

Dance in Atlanta in 1992 with the Uhuru Dance Company. I still remember how awkward it felt doing African dance though I came up dancing during the pop, lock and break dance era, which was really an extension of African dance. I went from dancing once a week to nine times a week over 6-day span.

I performed for the first time in 1995 for the grand opening of Life's Essentials Natural Food Market and Domiabra Vegetarian Palace, my first restaurant experience. I would take classes with some of the best of teachers including My Baba and Iya Ile Company founder, dance, culture and spiritual teacher Kwame Ishangi, (Ibaye), Marie Bass, Yusef Kombasa, Assane Konte, and Babacar Ndiaye. I would continue to perform while with Harambee Dance Company, in New York, as well as with the African American Dance Ensemble with the Legendary Baba Chuck Davis (Ibaye). I took on the role of his God Son and he would be one of my greatest influences in dance, music, and song and business even.

I recall rehearsing for a big gig at the American Tobacco Campus, in Durham, and I was told that if I did not execute the choreography better I would not be able to perform. Where I was not going home and practicing as diligently as I could have, I made certain I did for the next 2 days leading up to the next rehearsal. My SSW was stronger because I committed to getting better fast.

I was honest with myself about it and was clear that I was not at all comfortable while in rehearsal. The combinations and steps, for this dance, which I had experience and familiarity with, were still complex and intricate. With patience and perseverance, I prevailed as a dancer of that piece. I knew I was going to make it before I walked into that rehearsal so I had already added value to myself before it was recognized by Asst Artistic Director, Stafford C Berry. This is important to note because I had to deem myself worthy of self-recognition just based on my standards of working hard. It was then subject to scrutiny by Baba Chuck. If they had said I was not ready I would have been disappointed but not lacking SSW. It is important to make that distinction.

I mentioned that SSW can have value added by not taking an action or not saying something. I celebrated myself tremendously in my mid-twenties when I practiced celibacy for over 3 years. I did this after recognizing how much drama was created by having intercourse too soon with sisters. I claimed that I had developed a solid friendship with these sisters prior to engaging in those activities. I had actually developed a strong acquaintance but not a friendship with them.

I had incidents with young ladies that my cousin Chase jokingly called, playing butt naked games (BNG). I would tell him about excursions where we might have slept in the bed together or even shower together but did not engage in any activities. I would not give in to any sexual urges. Essentially, I refused any and all sexual intercourse proposals until only connecting with my ex-wife and, after, my current wife. Back when I was abstaining, I said I would not have sex with anyone again until I could see her as the mother of my child(ren) and my wife.

As a male, I enjoyed BNG, but as a man, I was very proud of my discipline, self-control, focus, commitment and honesty with myself and these young ladies. It felt good to be wanted sexually, finally, by women. As a male, I was operating out of PSW but as a man, I was able to have enough semblance of responsibility with these women. I proudly say that the women exposed to me during that period got to experience a man raising the bar on valuing the sanctity of exchanging sexual energy. They got to experience a man rising above his physical desires even when the lure of a naked body was within arm's reach. Though I became very acquainted with the unfortunate concept of 'blue balls', it was worth it.

SSW includes not speaking aloud something that is being contemplated; especially when you know speaking on it is more about drawing attention to yourself. An example of not saying something as an actual means of adding value to your self is essentially any scenario where you wanted to, for example, tell someone off or curse him or her out but did not. The value of this action or inaction is multi-faceted.

I was on the bus with my Bredren I-Ras, back in my Clark Atlanta University days, when we lived in College Park. We were going food shopping near Greenbriar Mall in Eastpoint, GA. I was fresh from NY with a mentality that was misplaced. My attitude was, do not look at me hard unless you are bringing the drama. I was groomed to not back down. Mind you, I was probably a buck 25 at the time (125lbs).

I was not a troublemaker or a 'hard rock' by any means, but still, I was moved to inquire as to why this dude was clocking me so hard. He walked on the bus and proceeded to the back seat but our eyes met and locked pretty much the length of the bus. I initiated the disengagement and paid him no more attention until I was preparing to get off the bus. By this time I was standing near the rear exit door. Our eyes met again. I asked him if everything was cool, in an inquisitive manner and tone, as opposed to a confrontational tone, so I thought. I did not ask him so that everyone could hear because that would have been a blatant example of PSW. It was loud enough for him to hear me from the 15 – 20 ft distance he was to me at that point. He responded immediately by standing and approaching me with a silver plated 9mm handgun in his hand asking me if I had a problem with him.

Answering in the affirmative could have placed my life in more jeopardy than it already was so I decline to answer and just observed him as he paused for a moment awaiting my response. He then proceeded to back up and finally sat down with gun still in hand. If I had responded, that would have been an example of PSW because it would have been a result of me trying to have value added to me by the bystanders on the bus witnessing this play out.

They would have been able to say, "Yo! shorty is no joke standing up to that dude even though he had a gun and approached him right on the bus. Shorty must be a hard rock from New York ready to knuckle dude down". It would have been a story for me to tell on some 'I am not scared of anybody' tip. It was not a difficult decision to keep my mouth shut under the circumstances. What if I had a gun as well? Which version of self-worth would I have gravitated toward SSW or PSW? The purpose of this book is for you to ask yourself questions like these. Why did you do what you did? If you had made a different decision would it have been SSW based or PSW based?

We all like to tell stories about how tough we are and how nobody should ever think they can get away with 'punking' or disrespecting us. Think about things you have done that you could not wait to tell someone about. Those scenarios often have PSW written all over it.

This idea and practice of not saying something is underrated as a means of adding value to yourself. You realize how valuable it was to not speak on something usually after the situation plays itself out. SSW is about being in control of yourself and your emotions, whereas, PSW flourishes with emotion and reaction. Think about when your mate wanted to discuss something that you were way too emotional to speak about. You knew it would not end well so you requested to hold off on the conversation so that you could actually reason on the matter instead of arguing. Now, be clear, arguing is replete with PSW because your goal is to win the argument.

People love to argue because it is a great way to have value added to them, not from their adversary but, by the people they are going to tell about the argument they won. The adversary is only a source of adding value if and when they humble themselves and admit that you won the argument. Please think about where you fall or reside in this conversation of speaking for the purpose of building up your value.

Anytime you wish to 'slap the taste out of someone's mouth', you are at a crossroads of SSW and PSW. If you are willing to do it in a private setting without sharing it anyone after, you are within the bounds of SSW. Maybe, this is the time you finally stand up for yourself. It is more likely to be SSW if your intention is to elevate and improve the person and not disparage or embarrass the person. This is another indication of your self-worth agenda as it relates to involving other people. SSW is about elevating and celebrating yourself. PSW is being highly regarded and celebrated by others accordingly.

Anytime and every time I was without a car, as an adult, I contended with how I would be viewed while walking up and down the street or waiting for the bus. These times are always humbling because I always play this game where I would ask myself if I would drive certain cars that passed by. These cars might be rusty, old, badly dented, without a bumper or even the Pontiac Aztec, but I would always say yes, no matter what the vehicle. Yes, I would even drive the visually unappealing Pontiac Aztec.

For various reasons, I had to reside to riding on the bus as my primary mode of transportation. During this time, I had to question what impact it was having on my self-worth. I had to constantly talk myself through not allowing my mode of travel to speak for my worth. Most recently, I felt great about it! I practically wrote this book while on the bus. I felt tremendously accomplished so my SSW was on the rise. I obviously did not have enough money to get my car fixed or get a new car. This situation still did not adversely affect my self-worth.

I could not allow my self-worth to be equal to my financial situation at that time. This is the mistake we make quite often. I am often reminded that the situation could be flipped such that I was driving a full-size luxury SUV but have little self-worth to celebrate or reflect upon.

The more I think about it, the clearer I become about how everything we do including breathing in a controlled manner has the opportunity for us to feel great or greater about ourselves. I devoted this chapter to giving you and reinforcing for you the concept of assessing the source of your self-worth. The rest of the book takes you through different areas of life where self-worth building opportunities exist.

Moving Forward

I have worked 3 jobs as an adult. In all cases, I have recognized that there has been a common theme that interfered with the maximization of the progress and success of those businesses. They all lacked effective systems for communication and honesty with self and others. This book means nothing if there is little commitment to self to be honest while communicating with self about every move we make in life.

I offered a recap of memorable events in my life and moving forward, I ask you to reflect on your past memorable events and situations. Look at your overall self-worth and assess the source and whether it is pseudo or sincere. You may care about what someone thinks about you even when they have no control over a life circumstance of yours. It is a problem if we put too much energy in those people, whoever they may be. Looking good and feeling good about your self is essential. What you are willing to do or sacrifice to look and feel good about yourself, offers contemplation about your self-worth. Move such that you can look at your naked self in the mirror and love the shell as well as the core being.

Chapter 2

Birthing and Building Self Worth

The self-worth of a child can actually begin at conception or at the point where the parents are aware of conception. There are men who feel accomplished simply because they are not 'shooting blanks'. This could be pseudo or sincere. The woman can justifiably celebrate her body functioning in the manner that allows her to conceive. Since women usually do not brag about how many babies they can have or how many times they have gotten pregnant I consider this both sincere and celebratory. Both cases can represent the parents adding value to their respective selves as well as to the baby.

The manifestation of self-worth in a baby seems to really take off at the moment they are able to do things on their own, such as when they learn to use fingers effectively, eat, crawl, walk and dress themselves. Basically, anything that we seem to celebrate for them doing, they then celebrate for themselves. As children learn more about what they possess and what they can do there is an increase in PSW development.

My 3-year-old decided everything was hers. She claimed cell phones, computers, food, adult clothes and beverages of all types. Somehow, children got the idea that possessing more seems to make you important. She loves flowers but they also had to be claimed as possessions. She would tell us to look at *her* flowers as we took walks. If I asked her to bring something to her mother, she would, 'look what I have', instead of saying, 'Bey Bey told me to give this to you'. This same 3-year-old also suffered from a lack of humility. She would be in the most vulnerable state and would still resist being told where something was, or how to put something together.

If her Mother or I would fuss at her for something she would cry louder and never would acknowledge that she understood what we were saying. Me: "Do you understand why I said stop standing on the futon? You could slip and fall" Her: (while nursing her wound) "no". She was not going to be wrong! The devaluing that comes with being wrong was already real for her. How many of us adults feel devalued by being wrong? Or by being checked? Or advised on how to do something better?

My daughter then figured out a way for us to no longer fuss at her, no matter what she was doing or about to do. She would politely escort us out of the room or area where she was. She would tell me to go to the kitchen since that is where I spend most of my time. She would Shsshhh me with the finger to the mouth and all, when I attempted to check her. She would respectfully ask us to not talk to her, please.

As funny as it may have been at the moment, if this goes unaddressed, she will grow up with these same tendencies. Please think about how many adults you know who still have these same traits of refusing to be corrected. Please consider where you put up your wall or creatively get out of hearing critique, guidance or advice.

She still has a long way to go toward displaying that needed humility as an adult. You must possess humility if you are to remove yourself from the clutches of Pseudo Self-Worth. She was not trying to hear anyone's assessment or perspective on whatever the situation. She will literally attempt to talk over you so that she does not have to hear you.

My teenage daughter, while at her 3-year-old Born-Day celebration, played in her playhouse in the backyard for several hours by herself. She continued to play alone even while her friends and guests were all over the yard and house playing and enjoying themselves. At a certain point, she decided to go into the house and to her room. She was so upset when she saw other children in her room playing with her toys. She immediately claimed everything as hers and tried to take everything from everyone. We see this happen all of the time with children.

As soon as children see another child with something of theirs, they immediately want it and their position is, 'it is mine and I want to play with it now'. I did not make the connection between this behavior and PSW, but now it is clear how this behavior is emphatically indicative of the presence of PSW. How many times were you interested in being with someone only after you saw them with someone else?

Now maybe I am being a little harsh on these cute and innocent toddlers, but what happens when you continue to see it and more often as they get older? The preschooler and pre-tween will add bragging and false claims into the mix to bolster themselves up some more as a ploy to get recognition from their peers and others. As you reflect on these scenarios you will see how PSW is easily identifiable.

Have you ever tried to tell a child something and the first thing they say is 'I know' even though they obviously do not? Not only that, but they barely let you get it out before they tell you they know. I have one little dude who will tell you about something that maybe you did not know to balance out you telling him something he did not know.

My friend purchased a new car and his daughter leaned on the car proudly as friends were dropping off their children, for the function. Her intent was to add value to herself, by way of the car purchase made by her parent. She made certain every child saw her on it, cementing her PSW for the moment. Another child immediately started talking about everything he knew about that car to display his familiarity with it. This was his method for getting in on the PSW fray, and not being outdone.

In being honest with myself, there are some children I do not like being around. In being more honest with myself, I have to acknowledge that I chose to be irritated because I see my reflection in them. Their PSW agenda is always at the forefront of their interactions with others. That is why I get so excited by a child who has a sweet demeanor, is pleasant, polite and helpful. Children who know early on, that their purpose in life need not be about proving something to others is my favorite type of child.

As parents, sometimes we call ourselves empowering children to be themselves at a young age. That sounds great and may actually be a deterrent for PSW but it can often backfire. If a child thinks he or she has the right to express him or herself and they are not 'properly trained' it may come off as disrespectful and provide a source of PSW instead of SSW.

The goal is to have the child feel great about who he or she is and his or her contribution to the home and social environment. When this child feels good about him or herself because of the interaction and the impression left on the adult, SSW has an inviting comfortable place to nest.

Children have significant needs. As babies, their basic needs must be met. They must be clothed, fed, changed and energetically cared for with smiles, laughter, kisses and talking or singing. As they get older it appears to us that they do not need as much, but I am convinced that they do. Though it seems that we are not as important while they have become more self-sufficient and more interested in games, electronics, friends, and media, they still need time and individual energy from us the way they used to receive it. Their self-worth depends on our time and energy spent with them. Our children feel more valuable and vulnerable when they experience these displays of love.

PSW would drive them to; for example, act out in school as a means of getting attention. Parents may have to then leave work to pick these PSW carrying children up from school because were suspended for bad behavior. When these children are asked why they did what they did, they respond, most of them, most of the time, 'I don't know'. That is because they do not know. They are unable to articulate why they are doing what they are doing or not doing. This is one of the rare times when it is understandable for child to 'not know'.

There is a new phenomenon, at least new to me, of not turning in completed school work. My oldest daughter is a fan of this rave. She does not offer an explanation for her inaction of turning in the work but she has clearly done it. But is this also an attempt to get the same attention she was used to getting when she was the only child and I had more control of my schedule?

Children learn the most from us and what we expose them to. We say things like, 'children are the future' and we sing the song "The Greatest Love of All", but we do not capitalize on the opportunity to maximize their sincere self-worth. "Show them all the beauty they possess inside. Give them a sense of pride to make it easier" This is what we are not effective enough at. They have to find their own way and in doing so they focus on doing things that get the attention of others, young and old.

They are acting out because of our negligence in recognizing their feelings of inadequacies. "Remind us how we used to be". When we all operate out of PSW it shows them how to operate. We see them but refuse to see the reflection of self so not only do we not recognize that they are adding a false sense of value and pride to themselves, but we have been and are doing the same thing.

We miss the opportunity to catch PSW behaviors and tendencies partially because we think these toddlers are too young to guide. We allow things to play out saying things like, "they do not know any better". They may not know better, which is why we need to be vigilant sooner rather than later. Once that behavior sets in, it will be more difficult to reverse it, especially when it is the social norm. It is normal and commonplace for people to act out of a place of PSW.

It may be just an irritating trait your child exhibits but, left unaddressed, it can and will develop into a PSW mess. They will claim and speak of more 'things' to celebrate. These may be bigger things, brand name things, more expensive things and things that belong to someone else like parents, siblings, extended family members and friends. Anyone will suffice as long as they can get credit for even speaking on behalf of … these items. Again, these are things that are not even theirs but there is value in being associated with the possessions or success of friends, family or hometown sports teams. They will scream for your attention in the most subtle ways. We will fuss at them, shout at them, pluck, pop or spank them and they will rejoice because they have that attention they sought.

Moving **Forward**

Children must be celebrated enough to know how to celebrate themselves without the applause and endorsement from others. If anything, they must be taught and trained to do their best such that they can applaud themselves. We have to remind them to celebrate themselves and show them how we do it. Children have to be called out when they are looking for attention from others as a means of being worthy. Children must know how to handle their own self-worth account. They must be acquainted with the question as well as know the answer to, is your self-worth pseudo or sincere?

Chapter 3

Self-Worth at a Most Crucial Time, Young Adulthood

The major component to consider with the 13 to 17 age range is the fact that they have something to prove to themselves and to everyone else. If you know a teenager you have probably recognized this. Teenagers are preparing for the rest of their lives with critical life decisions to be made. Simultaneously, they think they are ready to have sex, drink, smoke cigarettes, ride the transit system alone, go to house parties, stay out later and later, and hang out with whomever they deem worthy. We know they are not ready, but what we think does not matter to them.

The teenager can be a most complex individual. Most of them wear their attitudes with pride. They have grown and become responsible in so many ways yet are often more irresponsible than anyone can believe. As budding adults, teenagers are maybe the most susceptible to the pitfalls of Pseudo Self-Worth. The social component of high school certainly feeds this stage as well. High School offers a concentrated gathering of individuals vying for value imposed by others, PSW.

Now you may have a really grounded young person to the extent that they are respectful and possess an upbringing replete with lessons of self-love first. Your teenager may have bought into the practice of being a leader instead of a follower. If this is not the case, they will struggle every day to reach the standards of others with their hair, dress, footwear, talk, and behavior.

I was a grounded teenager, relatively speaking. My parents legally separated when I was 6 years-old and divorced when I was 12. I lived with my mother primarily and spent my weekends with my father. Both parents encouraged me to focus on me and not what others were doing or possessed.

With that said, I remember when my father gave me $100 for my 16th solar return. I already knew what I was planning to do with it, buy a Ralph Lauren jean jacket from Macy's, full price. It did not last two months before it was borrowed by a friend and lost. I was kicking myself for essentially wasting money on something I bought just to draw girls into me, and have dudes envious of me. I recall purchasing a pair of Ralph Lauren Moccasins that had a red, white and blue patch of leather that I really disliked. It was a designer shoe and that was all that mattered. That was my last Ralph Lauren purchase and that was prior to learning about his lack of regard for my community patronizing and supporting his brand.

I had a Liz Claiborne denim jacket that I had never seen anyone else wear. I was replete with PSW because I was the only person with this style of jacket. That was lost after a period of months as well. When I was wearing it I used to hang a 5 inch Ernie doll from the zipper. I did this because My S-Curl made my hair look like his and I was working on a gimmick to attract the ladies, once again and just stand out from the crowd. I was even looking to rock a shirt like Ernie to add to my originality, I mean PSW. Whatever you wish to call it, it had nothing to do with who I was but rather who I was trying to impress and what type of attention I was trying to get.

    I had the New Balance tennis style sneaker with the blue and green stripe to match the blue and green Gucci suite Erik B and Rakim had on. I purchased everything those colors to match my one pair of fresh kicks. I was in to low budget shopping, so I would hit Century 21, BFO, SYMS, Secaucus (NJ) outlets and the Macy's marked down section. But, again, I did it all to attract girls and compete with dudes, which would add to my PSW. My efforts were futile. I was not 'macking' by any means.

    I began drinking alcohol when I was 13-years-old. The corner bodega had no issue seemingly selling beer, coolers, and Cisco to minors such as myself. Granted, I pretty much only drank with cousins, and I was always close to home, but I passed out several times and had plenty of hangovers at a relatively early age. This continued through high school lightly, but then picked up when I got to college. My housemate and I would have alcoholic beverages every Friday and Saturday night, just because. We made 'the mix', which included any cheap vodka, kool-aid and Mad Dog 20/20. I finally stopped in my early 20's but I remember acting a certain way while intoxicated. I remember proudly speaking of my drunkard experiences, reflecting my pseudo self-worth tendencies.

Generally speaking, the humility factor of a teenage is quite volatile. It is difficult to simply have a conversation with them where there involves an offering of guidance or advice. These folks are convinced that they have seen and know enough such that they can navigate through the pending life experience well without another round of input from you. If they admit to needing your feedback, then it may substantiate your need to dictate and 'control their lives'. The teenager cannot afford this perception to manifest. They get PSW value from doing things on their own, in hopes that everything will work out alright. This has been my experience as a teenager, as well as by observing them.

With the advent of the technological progressions, these teenagers have access to things we could not even fathom while in our teenage years. (I am in my late forties.) They have at their disposal; cell phones, tablets, laptops, desktop computers, watches with video and online capabilities, game consoles with online capabilities, hot spots all over the city and even personal hotspot devices that can travel wherever they go.

With this technology they can stream videos and movies on Netflix, Hulu, Youtube, Vimeo, Dailymotion and World Star Hip Hop, just to name a few. They have unlimited access to view sexual intercourse and activities, drugs from growing to cooking and packaging, to using guns and their deadly effects, vulgarities, displays of disrespect, violence of every nature and music videos, which perpetuate PSW in a thorough fashion.

As a youth, I had never, in any movie or television show, seen blood splatter from someone getting shot they way we see blood and guts today. That all changed when I was a teenager. Now, because of desensitization, 'games rated mature' which include sex, blood spilling, and drugs are the most popular video games. We are proud to play and be associated with these games because they bring attention and status.

The fact that we are allowed to play these games add value to our PSW account.

In my beloved Hip Hop community movies are very important to the culture. There is emphatically a PSW component to bolstering movies like Scarface, The GodFather, and The King of New York. "You never seen bank like Frank White", is a popular lyric from Notorious B.I.G. emulating and celebrating the gangster of that movie. The biggest of the PSW builders are 'money, power, respect', 'sex, ho's and clothes', but essentially 'it's all about the benjamins'.

I was a teenager during the golden era of Hip Hop. I had access to the originators of hip-hop right on through to the innovators. I wanted the blue and green Dapper Dan suites Eric B and Rakim wore on the cover of the Paid in Full album. I wanted a four-finger ring and a nice chain, but not a 'dooky' rope chain. That was asking to get robbed.

I remember the cover of Criminal Minded with the gun and ammunition. I remember wanting money, cars, jewelry, half-dressed woman surrounding me, rolling with and feeling on me, sneakers, Timbs and I wanted to dance in videos. This was all PSW imposed. Granted, I loved to dance and still do but I wanted to be seen. I got none of those things but I still manage to celebrate myself every day, sincerely. I felt good about myself, but I gathered I would feel even better with those added perks.

Back in the day, I knew of marijuana as 'reefer', 'a joint' or 'cheba cheba' but did not know what getting high was. I knew nothing, absolutely nothing about cocaine or heroin. Whatever I did learn about had to happen right in front of me, which is way different from today. Today you can see a joint rolled up, a line of coke sniffed or a hit of Heroin injected clearly into one's veins on all forms of media. For so many getting high is just as much about letting people know, as it is actually doing it. Remember that when you are prone to broadcast your behavior, thoughts, and activities, you are fast approaching PSW status.

My siblings and I once smoked my father's leftover cigarette butt or at least tried to. I was 7 at the time, and what I remembered was that I coughed intensely and NEVER picked up a cigarette again. There is a documentary called The Tobacco Conspiracy, which talks about, among many topics, one of the marketing ploys to increase tobacco use. They targeted the self-worth of the population and emphasized how 'cool' you looked when you smoked cigarettes. Even when the industry and government knew of the harmful effects of smoking, they catered to our PSW as a major means of getting the population addicted and catapulted the industry simultaneously.

I had a picture of Jayne Kennedy on my wall from the age 13 till I left for college. She was pretty. That was enough for me. I did not think to look at her breast, her hips or her butt whenever I saw her in movies. My exposure to sex was rudimentary and minimal. My favorite movie for a while was about the Dallas Cowboy cheerleaders. I am certain it had something to do with the half-dressed woman, which was still nothing compared to what teenagers see today. I could appreciate beauty without striving to attract it or them to me. Nowadays I am wondering if the AXE commercial ads are true: I wonder if woman will find me irresistible and mob me every time I leave the house because I used that product. Not to worry, I am sticking with my unique oil blends.

No longer is it enough to just appreciate beauty. From a PSW perspective, dudes need the attention to confirm worth as a man. So the question becomes, 'what can I do to get more attention from the ladies', to add value to my PSW account. I am clear, in being honest with myself, as a teenager and to date, what woman could do to add to my PSW. If women I thought were attractive, and maybe even some I was not as drawn to, would shoot me a smile or brush against my hand or another body part, especially unsolicited, I would feel GREAT! But, I am aware, it would have nothing to do with my spiritual self, or me living out my purpose, It would be a reflection of my physical possessions or my clothes or even my locks, but not me or my SSW.

I spent many years as an HR professional and had to deal with Sexual Harassment training often. I sat in on terminations due to harassment and had to participate in investigations for the organizations I worked for. In this unfortunate period of #metoo reflections, where women are sharing that they too have been sexually harassed, assaulted or made to feel uncomfortable in work and non-work settings, I am certain that PSW plays a role in this. I have always been too concerned about making someone feel uncomfortable to give in to my PSW issues, but I know how easy it can happen. All it takes is a needless compliment in hopes of getting a smile in return. A manager can feel be PSW fulfilled even though the energy they received had nothing to do with their appeal, smile, jewelry, car, house or watch, simply the power they had to make a decision. PSW is not the only motivation but it is a key motivation in these scenarios.

Teenagers are under the impression that if they have sex it will magically make other things happen. They think people will value them more. They think people will want to be with and around them more. Teenagers think people will respect them more. They think they have power and can control people. All of this may be true under the heading of Pseudo Self-Worth. It will not mean any of those things. Teenagers, please wait on the sexual energy exchange.

I stated at the outset of this chapter, teenagers are at a super vulnerable stage as it pertains to PSW. They are deemed as having an attitude quite regularly. My estimation is that the attitude is rooted in, among other things, an inability to effectively display what they can do. They, just as we adults, are fighting to build and refine self-worth. The mere idea of being 'grown' has self-worth weight to it. We use it as a point of celebration or as a point of humiliation. "You think you are grown!" or, "you think you are grown?" are things that we, as parents, guardians, teachers or people in authoritative positions say to teenagers whenever the opportunity presents itself.

I recall experiencing my first love back in high school. It began when we met by way of another girl I used to like. I was 9 and you could not tell me I was not in love with this sister. She was a good friend of my love-to-be at the time. I believe it was the 6th-grade glee club that got us closer. She had a boyfriend but she agreed to have me as her prom date. This should have been a red flag but I was 'geeked' that she was my date.

I was supposed to keep it a secret but whomever I told allowed it get back to the boyfriend. That created a conflict for them but we were still going to the prom so I did not care about how they resolved their situation. We went to the prom together and we won the dance contest. This story is important because I was not trying to hear my mother when she saw us getting close in high school and recommended that we slow down.

The story picks up in the 11th grade when we became boyfriend and girlfriend. We both lived with our mother as the primary parent. We both were pretty focused on doing well in school and we both were comfortable enough with who we were respectively that we did not get caught up in anything that we did not wish to, relatively speaking. I say that but I was the rendition of Eddie Murphy doing his 'Okay' bit from Raw, the stand-up comedy routine. This was the routine where men would give in to their woman's needs and demands and say 'Okay' in a submissive manner. She and I were drifting apart and we actually broke up during the cab ride, the night my cousin Sean-Love and another mutual friend were all performing at the Apollo Theater.

The night was ended cool and we took a cab home together. We both lived in Lefrak City so I am sure I walked her to her door, and then went home, single. I do not recall how long it was before we connected and she expressed her desire to see us together again. I decided to accept her offer of reconciliation even though it went against my better judgment. I did it to appease her more than to address my needs, which included less drama. When we do things for others like stay in relationships, and it does not bring us joy, our self-worth has been compromised. I would do this for another decade before addressing this tendency as an adult. I still have challenges in this area.

We would last a couple of months before breaking up again in April. Valentine's Day did not go well because I did not do a good enough job of planning something more romantic. And I was not wrapped up in her the way I used to be. We double dated with Sean Love and his girlfriend at the time, (RIP LD). She was my first and last valentine. I was never able to pull anyone in for that 'helladay' and when I finally had one I did not want to be with her or engage in the charade. Valentines Days, for me, was another big PSW opportunity. It was a way to show the world who loved and valued you. I finally decided that this day had nothing to do with my worth.

It was a valuable 'first-love' experience and I value for her contribution to my journey. I learned a lot from this experience including what I think it means to be in love. Teenagers need to know that we can relate to them because all they have are their feelings to go on, so they think. We have to teach them what role they play in creating those feelings and ideas. This means, of course, we have to be accountable for what we have created in our lives including our feelings. Every waking moment offers us an opportunity to assess our self-worth and whether the value added is sincere or pseudo. Teenagers need this conversation so as to put into perspective what they are processing unconsciously but regularly. The teenager will have had the stage set to be great or will be busy trying to prove how great he or she is. Being accepted is the most common theme associated with this period in life. Simultaneously, setting oneself apart from the pack is yet another strategy to boost self-worth value in the name of being different. It is really being recognized for being different, which is a calculated effort to get attention. To seek attention is to seek the PSW value more often than not. There are teenagers who are actually different and feel great enough about it to comfortably display it. This is a win in the SSW column.

Moving Forward

A point of resolution for teenager self-worth challenges is to celebrate regularly their achievements and get them to take that same pride in it. Teach and show them by example that PSW serves no one effectively without exposing the true status of the SSW. It is essential that we, all of us reading this book, strive to develop and maintain a sincere sense of worth and value and not acquiesce to the standards and values of others. I am not referring to taking a job with a company who does not reflect all of your values. I am talking about compromising your values to win the favor of someone because it makes your superficial self feel good.

The more I write, the more I realize that we adults set the tone for what the children will regard as worthy to be deemed valuable. We can change so much in our lives and in the lives of the youth by building up our practical, functional and sincere self-worth.

Chapter 4

Real-Time Contribution To Self-Worth with Social Media

Social Media is a Pseudo Self-Worther's dream. It represents an unlimited resource for having value added to you by 'friends' and 'followers'. The apps leading the charge are easily identifiable as Facebook, Instagram, Twitter, Snapchat, Pinterest, and Tumblr. Remember, I am 40+ so the children may say Musicology as well. I just signed up for Snapchat and Tumblr while completing this chapter. I was leery about both of them because the conversation when discussing these two apps, in particular, was often referring to the heavily sexual explicit content experienced especially by young folk.

I would like to create a distinct disparity between me judging what people use these outlets for and my assessment of what I am seeing as it pertains to self-worth. Some folk wonder how such things could be posted on these media outlets yet other folks watch them and then speak of the disgust they felt. Some people cannot watch and will skip past it while others do not engage in social media at all because it is just too much of a distraction in their lives. And then there are the folks who actually post these 'disgusting, inappropriate, tasteless, tacky, violent, immature and seemingly thoughtless things. It does not matter what you post as much as it matters what you anticipated gaining from the responses. It goes the same for us and why we viewed what you posted. If we cannot wait to tell someone what we saw, beware of PSW and the attention getting component of sharing what we viewed.

When FB hit the scene I was often hit with 'how many friends do you have?' Compared to everyone I knew on FB, I had the least amount. I was not willing to put in any extra work to get more friends. My primary agenda was reconnecting with family, old friends and acquaintances. It was not to align myself with the seeming Pseudo 'self-worthers'. I think there is a fine line between posting how great you feel and spreading that positive energy, versus posting something to see how many likes and comments you get.

When I first signed up for FB I did more reading of posts than actually posting. I learned a lot about news stories and events primarily, and the movements and activities of friends secondarily. I was amazed to see postings like 'sitting in a tree reading' and then 127 likes underneath. At one point, I would wish I could get that many likes for something I posted. The part of me that envied the population of responses was the pseudo self.

In striving to be aligned with my highest sincerest self, I knew that if I posted about reading a book while sitting in a tree I might share my fear of climbing the tree and overcoming that fear or I might build on the book and how it impacted my perspective on something. I am also clear that I wanted to have so many friends that I would have to get a fan page, which might still require 5000+ friends. I am clear that my friend count does not reflect my perceived worth to the reading world based on what I am sharing or posting. I am glad to say that I have no clue how many friends I currently have.

As I mentioned in previous chapters, folks need attention, love, and a sense of knowing that they have worth in this life dynamic. If there is no awareness of the internal gifts that they possess then they will find something that gets the audience engaged and excited. Social media is the perfect opportunity for many to meet this objective.

A recent incident supports my position on this claim. A man filmed himself on FB killing another man. Now, in all fairness, this man had some mental issues as the assailant but before we learned he was mentally unstable we were disgusted that someone could post such a thing. I do not recall the number of views it had prior to being pulled down but it had plenty of views. We are a collective part of our societal issues by what we encourage.

I had a theory that dates back to the 90's that has now caught up with my position on PSW. We all have been delayed while traveling on the highway because of traffic. Here is what that scenario might have looked like. You complained and cursed, banged the steering wheel and otherwise expressed your frustration with these unexpected circumstances. You wondered what could be the cause of the delay. You are hoping it will clear up soon. You are doing the math to see how much time will pass before you will officially be late and if there is any way you can make up the time.

You finally see a clearing and your curiosity begins to build. You wonder what the cause of your delay was. You see smoke, a slew of police cars, an ambulance and 2 fire trucks. You immediately reach for your phone because you see an opportunity to record something that will be social media worthy. The wreck is horrific and you are steady recording or snapping pics trying to get just the right one.

When you post this pic, you may say something caring and compassionate like "I hope there were survivors from the wreck I took pictures of". You might say, "someone was probably texting". "We need to stop this and stay focused while driving". You may have even been emotionally reactive to what you saw and expressed that in some manner. Maybe you used a litany of emojis and symbols to display your sadness.

However you captioned your footage, you were that reporter trying to get the big story and win the glory from it no matter what carnage was left in your rearview mirror. If you were concerned about texting while driving you would not have snapped pictures or recorded the scene while driving. If you were concerned about potential survivors you could have saved your picture taking and recording and simply offered up prayer and progressive word sound and energy for everyone involved in the accident.

This was a perfect opportunity for PSW to rear its unproductive, insensitive and superficial face just to get some points. That post did not need to happen but we are constantly looking for ways to get value added and the phone and tablet are our new best friends. They make the magic happen to brings us our wealth of self-worth points. It used to be that we would make it to our destination and eagerly tell everyone about what was seen, but the phone removes the requirement to speak on it, just say upon arrival, 'Y'all gotta look at my post'. The funny thing is we already saw the post because we cannot put our phones down. We all are looking for opportunities to beef up our PSW and we never know what post is out there that we can like or comment on. We cannot take the chance on missing out.

If I owned a pair of brown and sky blue Clark Wallabies, I could see posting them on social media. The motivation would be for my 'up top' crew, Ghost Face fans, Wallaby connoisseurs and otherwise Clark enthusiast to celebrate and dare I say, sweat me. I would at least think about posting it but SSW is also about not submitting to PSW tendencies.

What I am clear about is, in being honest and aware, neither my kicks nor your likes, would make me a better person to anyone whom I care about. It does not make me any more committed to my highest self or possess any sincere value that will benefit the world around me. It really would make me want to do more and more to get the adoration and attention of others. I could go on and on about the postings I have seen that reek of PSW, but I am writing this book so that you can be honest with yourself about what you are posting and what you are celebrating. You can then answer the question for yourself, are you contributing to and adding value to someone's PSW? Are you looking for an external source of worth for your pseudo self? Just remember that the young adults are watching.

Moving Forward

I have linked up with so many folks who ditched the social media phenomenon fast because they experienced the focus factor, temptation and distraction social media was having on their lives. Let's see if we can post more education, historical, practical information instead of drama. Let's continue to share 'missing people' posts. Let's continue to celebrate those success stories and the children who graduate 4 years ahead of their scheduled grade level. Let's continue to post uplifting statements and phrases. Let's emphatically market our events, products, and services. Simultaneously, let's curb our appetite for attention and really challenge ourselves to take the time we would otherwise spend on posting and commenting, and take that time to do something we have needed to do for our personal betterment.

When I am working on this book and my FB notifications are on I will get easily distracted by that little box on the lower right-hand corner that pops up and tells me about something a friend of mine posted. I feel great every time I ignore it and keep focused. I do not always ignore it. Every moment can be a SSW moment or we can fold and make it all about what people will think of us. Social media is an excellent resource but it cannot be used only to fuel our PSW.

Chapter 5

Is your Self-Worth Driving you Mad?

Most folks learn how to drive as teenagers. I did not learn until I was 22. Teenagers develop driving styles, techniques, and attitudes that will not change until family and friends challenge them to do or be better. Blasting music, switching lanes without signaling, driving while leaning to one side and using one arm, driving with the window down even when it is cold and driving with the seat leaned ridiculously way back are all common traits of young drivers focused more on looking cool than on safety and regard for other drivers, residents and pedestrians.

My assessment comes with decades of observations and reflections of self. The most important factor to determine how much worth you shoot for is based on what you are driving. If you put a teenager in a luxury car you are setting them up for a PSW fiesta. They will look in both directions at every light to say, 'yo check me out'. Personally, I love being cool and being sweated for whatever might be sweat-able about me. I am also clear, now that I am wasting time and energy by relying on that PSW activity to bolster me forward.

Let's say I see an attractive woman at the light next to me and she seems phased by my ride, my posture, my earring, my tattoo, smile and/or my 2 chains. Let's say she smiles at me and gestures for me to pull over. So she gets out of her car and walks to mine with a flowing long sundress and a lot of cleavage showing. I already cannot wait to tell my peeps what happened.

Now, she tells me that she would like to get to know me and gives me her number, or even better, she asks me what I am doing now. I sense that I could smash it now so I cancel whatever I was on my way to do and go back to her place. Better yet, we go right to her back seat after pulling the car around the corner to an empty parking lot. I do not have a condom but I cannot let this opportunity to pass me by so I go raw. After it is over, I get out of her car saying I will call her but that is probably not going to happen.

I feel great about myself, but that had nothing to do with who I am. I am not a better person because of this escapade. It had everything to do with what I possessed and what she found appealing, as well as, her hormonal state of being. PSW scores a point and SSW scores nothing. For dudes, the question to ask yourself is "if you could experience that every day would it be worth remaining in a space of superficiality?" I can appreciate a scenario like that happening but I already know that there is no ejaculation worth an STD, unwanted, unplanned pregnancy and a waste of my life force by injecting it into a random woman.

Though this can also happen while walking or taking the bus, it is highly unlikely. Another important factor for new drivers is the need for attention in the form of music. Most cars today come with a pretty decent audio system. There is a general rule that, no matter how booming your system is, you turn the volume down when you drive in neighborhoods that may not appreciate your music selections and/or volume.

I listen to hip-hop, reggae, r&b, political talk, NPR, sports talk, jazz, and house primarily. It does not matter what I am listening to, I feel overcome with a sense of discomfort if I roll up in any neighborhood blasting music. It is probably more acceptable and more expected when 'everyone' blasts their music while driving, parking or sitting idle while in that 'hood'.

When I blast my music, with the windows rolled down and I am in someone's neighborhood I want attention which will feed my PSW. I want you to hear what I am listening to, and, as a DJ, I want you to appreciate my selections. I want to see you bop your head, sing a verse or find some other way to show me you are feeling me by way of what I am playing. My PSW does not care that it may be rude, disrespectful and needless. What is ironic is we will pretend we do not care what people think about us blasting music, but that is the very reason why are insisting on blasting music. We want people to feel and hear our presence. We want to be in the consciousness of others even if it is not favorable. Such is the nature of operating out of PSW.

Let me go on record and say I love certain songs loud and vibrating my body. I have wired house speakers into my car audio system in an attempt to feel the bass I wanted to feel. I would love to have a banging system but at the point, I am doing it just to get attention, I am feeding my PSW and I need to retreat. This is especially evident when someone gets in the car with you. I am a DJ by nature so I want my passengers to have the best experience, with safety as my primary agenda. I will have music for different age ranges and modes and I will only blast it when they seem to be in a state of appreciation for the 'boom banging' effect. You can appreciate a great sounding system and play music loudly, and still, avoid PSW.

If the music is playing high at relatively high volume, but I cannot hear you, I am going to turn the sound down. I am amazed at how many people I ride with who will yell over the music when attempting to have a conversation instead of just turning down the sound. This also happens when you call someone who is in the car with the music blasting but refuses to turn it down.

This could just be enjoying their loud music, and that is all, or this could be enjoying loud music masked behind the need for attention that will never be admitted or confronted. There is no such thing as, "I just like..." there is nothing that we just like for no reason, there is, however, PSW issues that we have not come to terms with that ought to be explored. If we are going to be better folks, we have to be honest with ourselves and be willing to address ourselves and call ourselves on our stuff. The next best thing to being honest with self is to have a friend who can call us on our stuff.

There is one more component to driving that must be addressed and that is road rage. To whatever extent you feel justified in getting upset with another driver about their actions or inaction, it is fuel to the pseudo self to tell someone how you disagree with their decision making. We seek self-worth so much that we think everyone should think like us and do as we do, except when we make a mistake. In that case, we should be forgiven and understood. Road rage can come from any number of distractions or bad judgments.

The worst infraction comes from almost causing an accident. That will get you cursed out.

It may earn you the stare down. If you are lucky, you will only get a finger or a honk. You are justifiably upset at the point an accident is almost caused, but your reaction to the other driver is going to determine where you are with your self-worth. My tendency is to focus on understanding because I have been looking for the right cassette, cd, lip balm or whatever I felt was important enough to look for while driving.

I consider myself a careful and intelligent driver, yet I have caused or have almost been the cause of accidents because I was 'slipping'. PSW will trigger road rage and have us take advantage of someone's mistake and pounce on them accordingly. A source of road rage is making someone wrong and dramatizing it as a means of building ourselves up. It also provides a sense of power for the car behind you to have to rely on you to move over so that they can pass. We often equate the power to pass or allow someone to pass us with our self-worth.

Sometimes we will humble ourselves and allow them to pass by moving over. But often times we go faster to stay ahead of them or we might even slow down to show that we have power and are in control of the situation. That really makes them mad. I know you do it because I have done it and consider doing it every time the opportunity presents itself. I am merely a reflection of you which is why I can make the claims I have made about how we use PSW.

Being in control or having a false sense of power is synonymous with possessing a false sense of self or having PSW. When we are driving we get mad because the power that we have to control the roads to our liking is tampered with by other drivers. That is why we get mad and develop road rage on a deeper level. The drivers who remain calm, accepting and understanding are more likely to operate out of a place of SSW. Let's stop allowing PSW to drive us mad!

Moving Forward

Let's step outside of ourselves more often than not. We cannot always be the victim. We cannot always be perfect and therefore not accept responsibility when it is our fault. If we made a mistake and someone got upset with us on the road, accept that they overreacted maybe and be alright with it. We, sometimes, will get upset that they got so upset even when we apologized or in some way accepted responsibility for the misjudgment on our part. If we had not made the mistake they would not have had to react in the first place.

We cannot think that people are attracted to us solely because of what we are driving, how we are dressing, how expensive our shoes are or how fancy our hat is. The quality people are going to look past those things and demand more from us we must be ready to display honesty, joy, self-control, consideration, empathy, patience and the rest. As soon as the need to get attention is our agenda, we must pull up and refrain from the action in question. We must be safe and respectful and allow the SSW accumulation of wealth to sustain us accordingly.

Chapter 6

Sporting Self-Worth

I like watching sporting events. My viewing usually includes, but is not limited to; college and professional basketball, college and pro football, baseball, bowling, and tennis. I am selective with the use of the word fan (fanatic) because I cannot say that I get fanatical about any sport or team accordingly. I have felt this way about my fandom status for the past 20+ years.

I was passively groomed to like the NY Knicks, NY Yankees, NY Jets and NY Giants. My appreciation for tennis came a little later watching John McEnroe and Jim Connors go it at but climaxed with Venus and Serena Williams. I liked most of the Big East and ACC conference teams in college basketball. I even remember liking Penn State because it was in the next state over, from NY.

I was all over the place. I based my emotional commitment to a team on circumstantial factors such as a player(s) or a coach deemed to 'deserve' to win a championship. If I deemed a players' attitude or sportsmanship as unfavorable then I rooted for the other team or player. I loved to watch Dr. Jay play so I was happy to see the Sixers win the Championship back in the 80's.

I liked the Cowboys growing up because my father bought me a Cowboys belt buckle when I was like 6 years-old. I thought it was protocol for me to like them and make them my team. Little did I know, they were considered America's team. I remember getting sad when I was old enough to research how many Super Bowls they had lost and decided I did not like the Steelers because they beat the Cowboys in past Super Bowls. I also decided I did not like the Redskins because Cowboys and Indians are inherent foes.

I liked the Yankees especially because I had a Chris Chamberlain bat from bat day when I went to a Yankee game in the late 70's. I even made Chris Chamberlain my favorite Yankee because I had to represent him, meanwhile, I could not point that dude out in a line-up to date. I understood, as a youth, that this is how this fan thing worked. I liked Reggie Jackson because he was deemed a great player and wished I had his bat instead. I remember my pride when eating a Reggie Jackson candy bar. It did not make me a better person or a better player but I became a fan, nonetheless.

I became a fan of Nate 'Tiny' Archibald after I read about him one day while at the library. I never saw him play but I envied him because I loved playing basketball and I was extremely short for my age also. I decided I would have a 'nice game' even as a short player. My SSW would benefit as I worked to be the best 5-foot player I could be. I do not condemn all fanaticism but I will continue to request that we scrutinize our behavior as it relates to sports.

I was a teenager when the 86' Mets won the World Series. I remember key plays by Mookie Blaylock, Darryl Strawberry, and Lenny Dykstra during that postseason run. I was so proud to be a NY resident even though it neither had anything to do with me as a person nor my contribution to society. I enjoyed the victory but it was not worthy of me pounding my chest with pride the way others did and do whenever 'their' team wins.

I was emotionally affected by Patrick Ewing and the NY knickerbockers being unable to win a championship after possessing such an exciting and talented team. I owned a pair of white on white Patrick Ewing's sneakers, which added to my commitment to 'my team'. I watched and discussed Knick games every chance I could. I was part of the heated debates and the intense discussions on what Oakley, Mason, Starks, Houston and the rest could have done against Houston in the finals loss.

In hindsight, I am amazed at how upset and bothered I got about those grown men losing, though they made millions and lived out their dreams. Meanwhile, I was doing very little in support of harnessing and developing my own skills, talents, and aspirations. My life was neither enriched nor enhanced by my infatuation with this these teams, these sports or the industry of making money off of fans who are trying desperately to possess some 'worth by association'.

I have to admit, further, that I cannot watch the 'big game' without having to leave the room if not the house. I cannot take it! If 'my team' is losing then I have to leave because the stress of them maybe not coming back from behind to win is way too much. I walked out on the Carolina Panthers in the second half when they played in the Super Bowl and lost to the Denver Broncos. This is because I live in the same state that the team is from. I get it! I know how it feels on the opposite end when 'your team' wins. It feels stupendous but it has nothing to do with you or how you are going to heal your community, or run your business more effectively, or be a better partner to your spouse.

If the team I want to win is winning and I start thinking about the fans of the losing team and what I am going to say to them, I know that I am in danger of representing PSW. Yeah, it is all in fun but is it? Are we really placing our worth as people in the hands of a football player catching the ball, a baseball pitcher striking out the side or 'Lebron' hitting a 3 pointer at the buzzer? Do not take my word for it: check it out for yourselves and lets blog about it after you come to terms with this PSW proposal.

The general concept when choosing sports teams is to go with the team that represents your hometown. The secondary criterion seems to be based on which team is most dominant and winning. I recall seeing Chicago Bulls fans born as soon as Michael Jordan joined the team. Whether people purchased Jordan's or rocked Bulls paraphernalia, they flocked to the team that offered an association with winners. Our PSW would have it no other way except to be 'on the winning team'.

Another PSW component to sports is in looking at the global perspective. There is an arrogance that the United States exhibits by suggesting that if you win the Baseball Championship, The World Series, you are world champions. The NBA finals are just that but we have claimed to have to possess the greatest basketball players in the world, i.e. Lebron James. I do not watch the Olympics like I used to while growing up, but I see the relative dominance of the US teams over the decades. That is when you can say you have a world champion, not just because you have a roster of international players on it.

The idea of liking teams and competing with others by way of 'who won the game last night' can certainly be fun. The fanaticism is on a whole other level when there are fights in the stands between fans of opposing teams. When teams win or lose fans are burning their neighborhoods down and flipping cars. People are arguing at work talking about "my team beat yours!" People are on high blood pressure medication and putting their health in jeopardy because some 19-year-old college Quarterback got sacked on the final play of the game, contributing to the loss of 'their' team. I find it ridiculous and a major distraction from major life matters. Remember, I talked about my 3-year-old claiming everything as hers as a means of adding to her worth in chapter 2. If we do not get the PSW in check we will continue the immature, reckless behavior as adults.

It is not practical to tie ourselves emotionally to something that we have absolutely no control of like the outcome of A GAME, yet we do it all year around. People go into depression when 'their team' loses the big game but make no connection between this reaction and the claim that they are having a 'bad day'. If we are talking about gambling, that is a different conversation but we are talking about Pseudo

Self-Worth and its adverse effect on our daily lives. I welcome you to step back and look at yourself as a fan or your folks and how hard in the paint they go for their team instead of for themselves or their family.

Again, my beef is not with sports fans, just people who allow their self-worth to be dictated by who they support in the sports world. We are better and more than who we like to see play on the court, field or canvas.

Moving Forward

Re-evaluate who your favorite team is. Your team probably can afford to be your household, your extended family, your community or employees. We conveniently select who we feel a connection with and team up with them accordingly. We make a connection with people who share; fan status, zodiac sign, hometown, taste in cars, a passion for Scarface, the latest hit single, or anyone on our side when another side exist. If you are from 'Up Top' then we have a connection deeper than that of someone from DC. This is a human tendency that pushes us further away from each other until we find a common enemy. In all of the alien movies we are a human race, but otherwise, we are our race, sexual orientation, political party, neighborhood or colors (gang). Let's make certain our passion is in a progressive place benefiting our highest self first and foremost.

Chapter 7

The Self-Worth Factor in Bullying

I went to PS (Public School) 206 when I was in the 5th grade. I experienced my first, and really my only bully. His name was Lenny and he was one of the class bullies. He was tall and slender, had curly hair and was brown skinned. Let me give you some related perspective. I was called French fry in kindergarten because I was that much shorter than everyone else. Not too much had changed with my height and size five years later. Lenny was one of two 'knuckleheads' of the class but Craig was relatively cool, which basically meant he did not mess with me.

Remember back in the day, when the schools would have those fundraisers where you would get your parent's friends to buy different trinkets and gadgets or pens from the small catalog, collect the money and then wait for the product to come in. Well, the product finally came in and Lenny tried to strong arm me into giving him some of the product. I refused Lenny's request but he found a way to get to it when I left the room. I knew he took it, but I could not do anything to get it back. He was much bigger than me and was about that fighting life that I was not a part of. I had to chalk it up as a loss and tell my mother that I could not provide any of the merchandise her friends paid for.

Here is the thing: I still remember that day and Lenny vividly even though that was over 25 years ago. Bullies lack SSW so they rely on PSW to compensate for possessing no real worth or value for themselves. He did not terrorize me day in and day out like some people experienced but I definitely felt helpless especially when the teacher did nothing once made aware of the situation. Lenny is forever etched in my mind which is one of the purposes of bullying, to feel relevant.

Bullying is defined as a person who uses strength or power to harm or intimidate those who are weaker. It is an ability to mentally traumatize others with fear and/or discomfort. If one is not affected or seemingly fazed by their aggression then the would-be bully is powerless and left to feel insignificant, until he or she finds another victim.

My oldest daughter experienced her first bully when she was in the 3rd grade. We are going to call her Sam to protect her identity. Yeah, you are right in what you are thinking, 'why did I tell you all about Lenny then?' Lenny stole from me and needs to be called out. If he can read and is reading this book, then this affords him the opportunity to apologize. Sam and my daughter had a different dynamic going on. I do not recall what set it off but Sam was more of a nagging, irritating pest always seeming to find my daughter as a subject of her attention.

My daughter told me about this girl who had been bothering her and I remember precisely how I handled it. Her mother and I were already divorced but we did a lot at the school to support our daughter and display our unity. I forget what it was called but there was a day when parents were invited to come and read to the students in the school library. While we were there I asked my daughter to point out the young lady to me. Now prior to seeing Sam, I recall explaining to my daughter why bullies bully. I explained to my daughter they are usually not feeling valued at home and are need of attention and love.

When I saw Sam my theory seemed that much more plausible. Sam's hair was relaxed (permed) but was a mess. It was still morning time so there was no excuse for her hair to be that messed up unless she left the house like that. She was a little overweight and had an unpleasant demeanor, which was easily noticeable in her facial expression.

So here is what I did: after the reading was over and the students began to line up I positioned myself to force Sam to have to walk past me upon exiting the library. When she was about to walk past me I tripped her. Just joking! I really did not do that. I did greet her by name, which took her totally by surprise since she did not know who I was. She asked me how I knew her name. I told her who I was and that my daughter and I had been discussing her. I flipped the energy though and told Sam if she ever has any issue with how my daughter treats her she should talk to me so that I can address it with my daughter.

    I made certain to greet Sam every chance I got to reinforce our relationship and make it less likely she would mess with my daughter again. I also wanted to recognize the young lady so that she could feel some worth. Children love it when older people, mostly the cool older children in the neighborhood, but sometimes cool adults or their classmates' parents greet and acknowledge them.

    Bullying has evolved so much. Now people are bullied on social media sites for everyone else to see. This is taking the PSW opportunity on social media and adding a subject as a means of getting that desired attention. This method of bullying tends to be highly effective because of our addiction to social media. I am always checking my FB page so if you bully me on FB it will be very difficult for me to avoid it. I cannot react to this attack the same way I cannot react to the driver giving me the finger in the next lane.

The best way to deal with someone's PSW is to acknowledge it as such while looking to strengthen our SSW. I explained to my daughter all of the reasons why Sam might value what my daughter had that she wanted, loving attention.

Child bullying is just one component of discussing this PSW matter. As I was listening to Notorious BIG and was reminded of the Gooch, 'the invisible bully', it shifted my mind to reflect on how mental bullying is as well. I almost forgot about relationship bullies.

Some of us get stuck in relationships where there is an emotional bully. I do not want to get too involved in the relationship conversation. Let me at least say, If you are with someone who is overbearing and a bully, but also, sometimes displays his or her appreciation for you physically, thereby feeding your PSW, it will be easier to accept this relationship bully.

There is no relationship worth being mentally or physically abused, but it happens far too often. This will be deemed acceptable subconsciously, at least, when PSW dictates one's value. If I do not think I can do any better than you and your bully of me, I am more likely to accept it. The folks who walk from that situation are the ones who are moving to sincerely add or recognize worth of self. They know that they do not deserve to be treated in this manner and will change their circumstances.

The bully in the relationship is in need of energy, attention, and power. This person is emphatically operating from a false and insecure sense of self. This person representing PSW offers a much clearer perspective on how detrimental this false sense of value can have on an individual, relationship, household, and society. It is only when they develop a stronger sense of SSW that the dynamics of the relationship can change. This situation can be much more destructive than one in the schoolyard or on the computer because the victim is sharing living space with the assailant and is trapped figuratively and literally sometimes.

It is important to understand the mindset of the bully and be prepared to battle mentally, not necessarily physically. After I typed the previous sentence I had a disturbing revelation. I can probably be deemed a bully to my children. It is especially the case with the smallest one, my now 3-year-old. I recognized my behavior when I picked her up and held her high up against the wall while attempting to get her full attention. I strive to intimidate her every time I apply this method of communication. My justification has been that my tactics are worth it because I need her attention.

So, yes, it is different when dealing with your children but is the premise, I am bigger than you so I can get my way, the best way to operate in our relationships. I suppose this is where spankings become an interesting conversation. I am far from having the personality of a bully but I suppose I have bully tendencies. I do not feel better about myself after the exchange is over but I do feel good if I get better results than my wife. My daughter is not spanked but she is overpowered.

This is that fine line I mentioned between PSW and SSW. I feel good about myself when I can give my daughter the look and get her to change her behavior, especially if this does not work as effectively for my wife. My goal is to change her behavior, not add value to myself, but I am on the line, by my self-worth building standards. I am not free of PSW, but I am aware of when it presents itself, empowering me to make changes accordingly. PSW is what has me competing with my wife about who has the most effective methods for dealing with the children, unbeknownst to her.

I have often felt like there are dog owners who take on bully tendencies. I have seen dog owners who love to yell at their dog and hit their dog for being disobedient. Of course, dogs need discipline just like a child but there is a difference that requires you to look at yourself honestly to determine if you are bullying your pet.

Moving Forward

Possessing a true sense of self-worth is essential in countless ways. Imagine a world without bullies. It is possible when one feels a great sense of worth. It is possible when one feels they are just fine even in the eyes and minds of others. It becomes problematic when one is being told that he or she is not good enough by a parent or 'friends' at school.

We have to start young and teach the children that the standard must not be based on someone else's definition of who is worthy. They must get reinforcement that reflects their beauty and value. These children will grow up to be adults but, without sincere self-worth, they will engage in violent acts in relationships, with the family and with strangers. They will engage in domestic disputes and abuse without knowing what the cause is. We will do anything to feel like we have some worth and if that means terrorizing others, we will do it. When we feel great about ourselves, we do not need energy or regard from others. We do not need to control others and we are more likely to celebrate our own Sincere Self-Worth.

Chapter 8

Am I worthy to be a part of this Religion?

Religion and spirituality are both essential to any civilization, nation, community, and individual. They offer a foundation to living and being. This chapter will address sincere and pseudo self-worth in a respectful manner while focusing on this invaluable and sensitive topic. The examples used in this chapter are in no way meant to offer judgment, disparage, ridicule or slight any religious group or spiritual concepts. I will share my experiences as I perceived them.

Every aspect of life provides a self-worth value-adding assessment but in this chapter, the stakes get higher when one's salvation is at stake. That is not the only reason why this chapter and subject is so important. Many of us are identified by our religion or spiritual philosophy. Our worth is in direct correlation with who we praise and affiliate ourselves with.

I will begin this important chapter in the book by reflecting on my religious and spiritual upbringing. I have no recollection of my father participating in any of our religious outings, which basically took place on Easter Sunday. My mother would go to church more often but would not insist that we accompany her. She practiced spirituality, but would go to church also. I used that language intentionally. Many people go to church to obtain or maintain spirituality. Her worship was a part of her spiritual expression but was not the source of it. My mother recognized and utilized the science of numerology and the alignment of the planets, Astrology, as a factor in what one's energy, personality or tendency might be. She also picked up on people's energy and she watched and listened to them. At that point it did not matter who you claimed to praise, she was assessing your behavior and actions or inactions. She could tell if your worth was rooted in your faith versus in your heart.

    I learned later in life that she recognized and utilized the power of persuasion as a means of influencing the subconscious minds of me and my siblings. She would talk to us while we were asleep, thereby programming us. In the Rastafari Culture that would be a reflection of Word, Sound Power.

    The use of words is essential in communicating with self and others. You might hear someone who is fully aware of words say, 'great dawning' instead of 'good morning' or 'morning greetings'. The morning is reflective of the sun rising and dawn surfacing. Morning, which rhymes with mourning, is not as favorable because of its vibratory relationship to the less desired mourning a loss of someone or something. In this instance, speaking and thinking are both applicable spiritual practices.

On one hand, one might feel a great sense of SSW because of the discipline associated with being more aware and intentional. Some may call this speaking or thinking positively which is certainly noteworthy especially when you have seen yourself improve in this regard. Using 'great dawning' instead of 'hello' has intention and purpose that 'hello' just does not have. Yes, it falls under the heading of being polite but does not act as energy moving you, or the recipient of it, forward. Saying 'peace' in place of 'hi' or 'bye' is another intentional means of executing a greeting or exit gesture. We feel better when we succeed in doing better, whatever that means for us. Feeling good about self is building and recognizing SSW.

PSW becomes the issue when you reprimand, criticize, scrutinize, or otherwise correct someone for speaking the way they speak. 'Conscious folk' (people who are simply aware of things) like to teach everyone who is 'in need of teaching'. Certainly, that can be a sincere gesture to inform and maybe uplift someone but it can also make us feel valuable because we have information that someone else does not have. If something is 'making you feel good', it is possibly synonymous with adding pseudo value. You may made me feel good about myself by spending time talking to me about talking more positively. I can celebrate the fact that you made time for me or I can feel good about having received your message and making better decisions because of it. You can experience both as the recipient, feeling good about the quality of the message and the quantity of time spent sharing the message.

The deliverer can feel sincerely grateful to have the opportunity to share the information that made a difference in his or her life and impart that wisdom onto another or they can feel bolstered by possessing the knowledge and disseminating it accordingly. They figuratively beat their chest or pat themselves on the back because they possess this information and 'people their insights'. Sometimes there is a thin line between SSW and PSW on these matters. The best judge of whether your thoughts and actions are on the productive end of the self-worth spectrum is you and your honesty with self.

In choosing my interactions wisely, if I come across as lecturing someone, I have less of a chance of actually being heard. I limit interactions and conversations with the folks who always feel the need to correct me or 'school' me on everything and anything whether it was related or not to the topic at hand.

Now with that said, I love dropping a jewel or two to teenagers and young adults but I keep it short. I respect that I am doing it for them more so than for me. I see it as a spiritual obligation to give to folks what was not offered to me at that same age. I had access to great adults in my teenage years but no one was bringing spiritual, historical information likened to what I am able to share at his point in my growth and development.

My first interaction with any religious affiliation was when my mother sent me to a Christian summer camp called the Word of Life camp. It was a two-week overnight camp in Upstate New York. She bought me my first Bible, which I still have 35 years later. It was my first time traveling anywhere away from my family for that long. We had church every day but we also had plenty of time for other activities like horseback riding and archery. Those are the two things I recall doing the most.

The most important memory of going to this camp was what happened this one night by the campfire. The whole camp gathered by a massive campfire and the camp counselors talked about getting saved and what that meant. Now, I had already been saved on two separate occasions but I felt like this experience might be different. The issue was, I did not feel different like I felt I should.

I went to church with my Aunt Mamie while spending many weekends with my cousin Sean

Love. Growing up, you had to have 'love' at the end of your name to add spice for the ladies. It was always all about the girls, ladies, women, honeys, etc. One time, I recall walking down the aisle when they called up first-timers who were ready to give their lives to Christ, and I said 'sure, that feels like the right thing to do'. I was never coerced by any adults in any of my saved experiences. I do think that was my first time getting saved. I am not recalling my second experience. Again, I thought I should experience some sensation that never came, which was why I gave it another shot, and then another.

    I was saved three times and, as aforementioned, I did not feel any different. I was not told that I should expect to feel different but I figured there should be a different feeling for such a tremendous soul saving accomplishment. Conceptually, it was also complex to anticipate that I had reserved salvation in heaven even while an inconceivable amount of sins were pending execution. Please note, I was 12 at this time.

    This is probably a good opportunity to add on to my religious and spiritual background, leading up to the present. I currently do not associate with a singular religion. I am very much aware of my spiritual self, operating out of this physical vessel, my body. I absolutely recognize that all of the areas I addressed in the first chapter when defining Sincere Self-Worth are fundamental spiritual concepts that permeate our being. The list includes but is not limited to the following: love, peace, joy, forgiveness, patience, discipline, honesty, respectfulness, respectability, service to others, commitment, gratitude, honor, responsibility, accountability, humility, empathy, caring, and nurturing to name a few. I respect energy and feel the spirit of beings and ancestors alike. I receive messages and communications from a higher source greater than this physical vessel I exist in.

By the time I was a teenager I was clear that I was spiritually inclined to deal with life experiences. I was a source of comfort for many people. They felt like I was easy to talk to and would, in turn, share intimate details without fear of judgment from me. I would listen often not knowing how I would respond once they completed their expression of concern, but knew I would be led to respond accordingly. I was not an angel, free from faults, nor am I today, but I was a virtuous person constantly looking to improve upon myself. That is still my quest and agenda currently.

As I moved through my teenage years I became hungrier for an affiliation to coincide with my spiritual base provided by my mother and harnessed by grounded family and folk around me. I would essentially look to expand my self-worth by selecting a religion/religious group that would reflect my spiritual state with doctrine and ritual. 'Self-worth by association' was conceptually birthed by way of the non-denominational Christian Church, The Worldwide Church of God (WWCG).

This 'self-worth by association' is PSW based, but is not always obvious. Self-worth by association is when you feel good about yourself simply based on who you know or who you are with. When you are younger you feel good about being able to hang with your older siblings, their friends, or the older children at school. As it related to this chapter, I wanted people to know I was a good person based on my chosen religion. My Aunt Sarah and Uncle Stan, whom I would spend a lot of time with growing up, were affiliated with this church for as long as I could remember. I went to some fun outings and met some really great people while at these events. My cousins, one older by 2 years, Stan (Ibaiye) and one younger by three years, Chasely, were mad cool to be around and they encouraged me to come to services with them in addition to the events, over the years.

In 1988, I attended the Festival of Tabernacles in St Petersburg, Fl. We went to services every day and I sat in and appreciated 'the word' offered by this new experience coupled with my spiritual hunger. I remember one sermon that talked about sinning is a sin even if it had not manifested in the physical form. If it was formed in your mind than it qualified as such, which provided an opportunity to develop and enhance mental discipline. I still recall the minister relating it to adultery and how, for me, viewing naked women and giving in to that lusting was just as bad as placing myself in the presence of a naked woman. I was just 18-years-old at the time and was nowhere near being married but it gave me something to consider for the future. The church was mixed and race relations seemed to be sound.

I met many girls, which was always going to be a perk of attending any event or function. In 1989, less than a year into my WWCG experience, my cousins and the friends I made from Brooklyn and Long Island, stopped in NJ to pick up some more friends and headed to Virginia Beach, VA for a weekend get-a-way with some female friends who lived there. That was when I met my now wife. I will expound on that dynamic later in the chapter. In bringing self-worth back into the fold of the reflections, let me express what I recall about who I was at that time from a SSW versus PSW perspective.

I had a high flat top, not quite as tall as 'Kid' from Kid-N-Play but noticeably tall. The trend back then was to put S-Curl in your hair just enough for it to straighten with a hint of curl. The Jheri Curl era was past so you definitely did not want to leave it in the full time such that your hair would curl up. The flat top with a fade hairstyle was big but if you had a curly top, resembling what was deemed good hair, you would get more play from the girls. I wore glasses with nonprescription lenses because it made me look smarter and that was also a trait the girls could appreciate, so I heard.

My job at the time and my church attire required dress shirts, slacks, and ties so I spent a lot of time in this area of attention-getting. I especially liked wearing 'feminine' colors like pink and yellow with socks to match my shirts. At one point all I owned were colored socks, all matching my shirts, and ties. The belt had to be Marithe Francois Girbaud, which was the indicator of good taste and money. I had the good taste but fronted like I had the money. I remember buying my first trench coat because that was also the trend and it made for a distinguished and professional look, especially accompanied by a briefcase. I purchased it from Mano A Mano, on Broadway just past Houston St in the Village, Manhattan. You could not tell me anything at that point.

My shoes were wingtips from the Bass outlet in Secaucus, NJ which I recall vividly because I never appreciated the look of wingtips prior to that period in life. I went years not purchasing any sneakers because I slid into this preppy stage of dressing. As I mentioned, I did not really have money like that so I learned how to cut hair as a means of keeping a fresh cut. Prior to that, I would get a cut from Mr. Green on Hancock and Irving for $4, which was a stretch financially back then. My church posse had two barbers in it but Khepera was in Hempstead, LI and Fel was further south in Brooklyn. I basically learned from watching and listening to them, especially Khepera since he worked in a shop.

I valued who I was as a person but did take notes to add appeal for the young ladies to consider me as a prospect. There were a lot of superficialities even though it was not as 'brand name' heavy as it was as a younger teenager. I do get credit for being one of the first to wear Tommy Hilfiger before his line hit the streets big. I have not thought about him, Ralph, Donna, Calvin, Liz, Francois or any of the designers who had me feeding my PSW as much as my budget would allow me to. It is amazing to me that these designers spoke out against my community wearing and popularizing their brand, yet we still gave and give them notoriety and financial support.

Going back to meeting my wife during that VA Beach trip, my SSW had a moment to celebrate. We all stayed at the host family's house where three sisters from the church and their mother resided. They knew my cousins and 'the posse' for years apparently, which is how we were able to stay there. We had a house party, which was great. I received a compliment that made me and my mother proud. I was and still am honored to have been told by their mother, at our departure, that none of the guests were welcomed to stay there again except me. Jokingly or not, I was recognized as the pleasant, respectful and relatively quiet guy I had always been. That was not the quote but I gathered that was in the neighborhood of what she said. I took pride in that regard and attributed it to my upbringing and relative commitment to being a grounded person.

I moved down to Atlanta later that year to attend Clark Atlanta University. I lived in a dorm initially but eventually moved in with my Aunt Charlene and cousins in Lithonia, GA. The Atlanta congregation was cool.

There was growth and development while attending that church, but I outgrew the doctrine and the culture of the church. I was amazed to find out that they were segregated while the country was segregated that continued even after segregation ended. I was told the by members how at dance functions blacks and whites could not dance together. If you lived in an area where you were the only melanin dominant person, you had to chair dance all night or dance by yourself. I am sure that sucked when slow jams came on. I began to have more and more distractions in services and within the church culture that propelled me past the WWCG and into, what was considered 'worldly', which was the world outside of the church.

I was still hungry, even more so, to have religion represent me. Again, I believed that if I were affiliated with the right religion then you would know who I am and how I move because everyone in that religion is upstanding and progressive. I had already moved to Atlanta to attend Clark Atlanta University and continued attending service there before my departure. When I left the church, I was indeed influenced by all of the new cultures and spiritual practices introduced to me in a number of ways.

I was listening to X-Clan which was visually and lyrically exciting to me. I remember the Kemetic, (Egyptian), theme and the emphasis on 'The Red, The Black, and The Green'. I saw the Ankh, the Kemetic symbol for Life, on their attire and posters, which intrigued me enough to learn more about it. I learned that the Ankh represented different things depending on who you were talking to at the moment. For some, the focus was on how it represented the man, woman, and children, family unit. For others, it was the full characterization of the female genitalia, the womb or uterus, the fallopian tubes and the cervix. I would listen with fervor to their music, which was even more culturally and historically in-depth than the socially and historical likes of KRS ONE, Rakim, The Guru, Wise Intelligent, Big Daddy Kane, The Native Tongue family and Public Enemy. Hip Hop plays a role in this religious and spiritual conversation, which I will delve more in to later.

Rocking it out to X-Clan led me to 'vibe' with cats who also liked listening to and appreciating their word sound. I remember building with Chaka Zulu, Current Vice President of Entertainment and Sports Marketing for Monster Cable, Inc. He was breaking down the term 'Vanglorious' for me. He also was a notable member of Phi Beta Sigma Fraternity Inc., the frat that was responsible for exposing me to most of our most prominent historians and scholars. Every Thursday night, they had a video series presentation that included the likes of, Dr. Frances Cress Welsing, Dr. Yosef Ben-Yochannan, Dr. John Henrick Clark, Ashwa Kwesi and Dr. Leonard Jeffries.

I was officially wide open. From this era in life, I became aggressive with reading especially on history, culture and other religious and spiritual practices. I had every intention of pledging Phi Beta Sigma Fraternity Inc, based on what they set off for me, but it was not to be so. While on line, I was told two weeks into pledging to cut my hair that night or do not come back. I did not go back. SSW or PSW? My locks represented something that I wanted my religion to also represent...me. Years later I cut my hair, but on my terms. PSW could have had me cut my hair so that I could be affiliated with them as a means of propping myself up. SSW could have allowed me to let my hair go so that I could be a part of this valuable organization to the community. This was a great time in my life. I had to make tough decisions.

My good bredren and, first apartment roommate, was on a similar path of growth and development. He came home excitedly one day with "The Isis Papers", Authored by Dr. Francis Cress Welsing and Neely Fuller, and shared that with me. Now, this era took care of my social, cultural and historical thirst for knowledge but I still had to feed the religious/spiritual piece. Dr. Anthony Browder's book, "From the Browder Files" blew up my religious foundation. By displaying how Christian origins were rooted in Kemetic history it really encouraged me to do some more research agin on Kemet.

My next book was the Autobiography of Malcolm X, which I saw that my older brother had read in years past. That was a magnificent read especially after having seen the movie X. I was open at this point to read about anything I had previously closed myself off to. The group I knew as Ansars, also known as Black Hebrews had literature for sale all the time when I was in Downtown Brooklyn. They were also present in Atlanta, at Five Points. I read several of their books. I went to Mosque number 15 congregating with the Nation of Islam with a couple of my bredren all on the path of elevation. I respected keeping the woman across the aisle because they can be such a distraction when spirituality is the focus. I really appreciated how their culture and religion got so many brothers off the streets and into the religion, into family and the community. I did not feel what I thought I was supposed to feel so Islam was not the religion I was settle in.

I read up on Taoism and was fascinated. It was so natural and logical and divine. I remember being excited by the simplicity and practicality of it. While saying and feeling this, I was clear that it was not all that I was searching for. I read up on Buddhism finally after hearing about it for so many years. It was an add-on to what I felt about Taoism, so it was a great experience but it was not all there was for me.

I attended The Shrine of the Black Madonna service as another means of exposure and experience. They had a big black Ankh on their place of worship which I related to my Kemetic studies with all of the scholars building on Kemet. I wondered what this could be because I saw that many folks had afros, and everyone dressed in red and black. The only thing missing was the green. I think that is why they had so many offerings. Listen, I know the Christian Church has plenty of offerings so it was not a judgment as much as it was a surprise. I appreciated the movement of the Shrine but I had $3 when I entered the building and I left before the 3rd offering took place, because I only had $1 left. I could not take the financial pressure, and I did not return.

    The Five Percent Nation of Gods and Earths was not new to me but the intricacies of it and its origins were new. I was not in the ciphers while growing up in Brooklyn and Queens. I vaguely knew what was going on when they discussed the mathematics of the day. It did not help to be dissuaded from associating with anyone who called themselves God. That was perpetuated by my specific Christian experiences as a teenager. I could have kicked myself for not seeking to understand their reasoning before making such an emphatic judgment of this culture. They were mostly young folk looking to work with a perspective that would produce viable building, reasoning sessions on how we needed to see things in the world other than how they were dictated to us.

    I became acquainted with the name Clearance 13x, the recognized father of The Five Percent Nation. I became aware of the 12 Jewels of Islam, the foundation of the Math for the day, and the alphabet. All of these concepts were practical and helpful in my growth and development. It further explained why I like Brand Nubian and Grand Puba, especially on the Reel to Real Album. As powerful as the Five was and is, I still knew it did not represent all of me.

Remember all of this searching is for me to relay to you who I am by way of my choice of religion or spiritual practice. What was happening though was I was learning more about my I-am-ness and what was and was not resonating with me. Something I did not mention but is very important to this conversation about self-worth is, I had to face family and friends who were still in the church. I walked with confidence regarding my spiritual growth. My self-worth was stable enough even while in my quest to be respectful and respectable, without a religion to wear on my sleeve. I approached the conversations about leaving the church as a non-judgmental move. I had to make the point that my soul was expressing it needed more and I was no longer in alignment totally with the teachings and practices of the WWCG to fill the need.

I had support from my mother, My Aunt and Uncle who I went to church with initially, my Aunt who took me in while in Atlanta, and all of my church friends. What was interesting was that as the years went by more and more of my friends from the church were no longer affiliated with the church. Everyone had a similar experience like mine where the alignment was no longer strong and stable. Everyone was on another spiritual path but no one had continued on the path of which we all met and grew together. It was mostly my generation. The generations ahead of us seemed to remain aligned and continued on the trajectory offered by the changing WWCG.

I already felt good about my movements but I was glad to hear that they recognized some inconsistencies that propelled them to better places spiritually as well. My SSW was strong and I did not need their approval or support but it was cool to have their understanding and support nonetheless. I would move on this path of perpetual growth expanding my reading to include Authors, Dr. Melofi Asante, Iyanla Vanzant, Susan Taylor and Ayi Kwei Armah. Books like Afrocentricity, Acts of Faith, In the Spirit and Two Thousand Seasons found nice homes on my bookshelves. My family who stayed in the church as it transformed treated me as a person not as a heathen so I had and have great respect and appreciation for them.

Another great thing about this period that had me feeling good about my growth and accomplishments was based on the suggestion that we read at least 10 pages of something daily. I proceeded to practice this every night before going to bed. I got to the point where I could not put books down and would fall asleep reading. When I first started out it was a challenge especially if I were reading something that required me to go back and reread to maximize understanding.

In late 1993 I started doing the Ruff, Rugged and Raw radio program on WRFG 89.3 with my good bredren I-Ras. It was in this time period where I learned about Rastafari Culture and felt like it might meet my objectives of effectively enhancing my spiritual self, based on my physical practice and affiliation. I was growing locks and past the fad phase. I respected that there was energy in my 3-year-old locks, which served as antennas to the universe. As I mentioned in an earlier chapter, the word sound power component was very empowering and effective. The message music associated with Rastafari was and is also irrefutable.

I will share the book that had the most significant impact on my spiritual development during this period: The Kybalion, written by The Three Initiates. What this book did for me was cement my eternal path of honoring, respecting and moving from a place of universal law. What it did for me was take me off of the journey to find that one religion, cultural and/or spiritual doctrine to represent my spirit. I saw that one religion could not represent who I was/am and will be, especially because I was/am constantly evolving and will continue to constantly evolve spiritually, which will continue to add new perspectives. That is what my path is and has been. This is not the same for everyone. I have accepted that and have found solace in that.

I used to honor the role of a missionary whose role was to help people find religion, theirs. I now value folks who have a regard for one's spiritual growth and development however it happens versus the potentially pseudo self-worther who insist that their path is the only path to peace, prosperity, and salvation. I had a young lady at the park attempt to recruit me just earlier this year, which I felt was unnecessary because, if she were actually paying attention to me she would have heard someone who was grounded, guided and humble. Even after I told her I have spiritual practices in place that move me forward, she said I do not really know if I need her church and congregation until I attend. And, of course, it is unlike any other experience I have had, in her words. Her PSW would have had value added if I had conceded to her will, but my SSW allowed me to respectfully decline knowing I would have been doing it for her and not me.

These examples are for me, please remember that. Some readers, who feel the same way about your congregation, religion, deity of focus may feel the same as this sister did. You may have someone still searching, and that would be the person who should attend your services, meeting, and gathering may be.

It is important to show respect for how people operate, otherwise, you may find yourself wanting them to think or be like you, which is a way to add self-worth to your pseudo self. In light of this last statement, I went to an Interfaith Seminary after I returned to NY and became an Ordained Spiritual Counselor. My goal was to make certain I had a diverse and practical understanding of the religion or spiritual base for anyone whom I might counsel. From a SSW perspective I am excited, and at a place of peace and comfort with my spirituality while still growing and evolving. I would continue on my journey which included learning about the African spiritual systems and honoring ancestors in a more hands-on manner. I am currently a student of Dr. Jewel Pookrum, OBGYN, MD, PH.D., and am in her brain balancing program.

These more recent practices supersede religion and focus on the same basic principles of discipline, patience, intention, and will, that I learned about and focused on over 20 years ago. For all that I have learned and continue to learn my agenda is not recruitment. You have to know what feels great for you which means you have to really be engaged in yourself. This is what having SSW is about. You know you better than anyone else and you are openly communicating with yourself about your movements. When you want to share your knowledge, which might be sound and exact, but you are doing it to inject yourself into the conversation to show that you have something worthwhile to share, it is PSW. It does not have to take away the value of what you would have shared but the spirit of why you were sharing it might have been tainted, neutralizing the energy of the exchange. From a spiritual growth perspective, that is an opportunity to not speak and give in to that urge. It takes awareness, honesty, and discipline, which will take that PSW event pending and immediately turn it into SSW. You will feel great about your achievement.

This chapter is one of the most important chapters because so much is riding on our culture, religion and/or spirituality. I know the value of all that I have learned over the decades. If you are living 'Christ-like' even without knowing who Christ is, you meeting the objective for a better life experience. Conversely, you might have folks who go to church as a devout Christian but actively, blatantly disregard the teachings. He and she may go to services every Sunday and bible study on Wednesday and Friday but still, lack SSW and pursue PSW relentlessly. The diligent studying of the scriptures is where self-worth is replenished but it seems to be more about what you know as opposed to who you are or what you do.

Moving Forward

I began this chapter addressing how I was looking for my religion or spiritual practice to define and represent me. I have offered some of my lessons and reflections as they pertain to my sources of self-worth through those years and the applicable experiences. I would discourage anyone from thinking that their religion, spiritual or social, cultural organizational affiliations define who they are. That would be another example of 'self-worth by association'. We all have PSW moments but I contend that SSW will have a more progressive impact on getting to and dealing with our true selves instead of that self that we want people to see and experience. We are not the church, mosque, center, spiritual house, temple but a vessel tapping into the energy from that space and place. We are there to raise our frequency and be our truer selves bringing us closer to the supreme energy source. Let us use our faith to build our Sincere Self-Worth.

Chapter 9

Is the food I eat worthy to be in my body?

There are only two things we do more than eating and drink, they are breathing and thinking. Ironically, we usually do not do either of these effectively when it comes to the eating process. We decide what to eat based on what is easy to access, convenient, habitual and in compliance with our sugar, salt, and chemical addictions, mostly. Our self-worth is so much a part of this eating piece. Now let's not make any assumptions about what I am getting at. You might be the person who throws down every time you enter the kitchen. You stick your foot in it every time and your reputation will be sound after your food is consumed. You might be a raw/live foodie or a non-discretionary carnivore. In either case, your food restriction or inclusion cannot alone be the source of your worth, if at all. This self-worth reasoning is so important because value added to your worth account manages to maneuver in and out of titles and classifications like vegan and carnivore.

Let me begin with some examples. SSW addresses internal achievements and goals accomplished while PSW requires the notification and celebration from external sources, so someone has to be involved in acknowledging what you have prepared or eaten. Just because we take pride in how good our food taste does not necessarily mean we possess SSW with respect to what we eat. Just because we are vegan does not mean we move with a strong SSW. It does not matter if specialty meats, like bison, ostrich, and chipmunk, are a part of the eating equation, because your self-worth is bigger than just your selection.

I am considered a vegan. I made the choice to eat plant based because of what I have learned and accepted about meat, poultry, fish, dairy, and eggs. When I had high LDL cholesterol levels, it was during a vegetarian phase where I surrendered to the cheese temptations. When I stopped eating the cheese my LDL levels went down. When I drank dairy I had more mucus than when I did not. I stopped eating fish when I learned about the mercury content of many fish I ate and was regularly available to me.

When I learned my favorite and cheap fish was farm raised with genetically modified ingredients and GMOs might be linked to cancer and the surge in food allergies, I decided I could live without fish and might live better without it. When I learned that the chicken I was eating really was not real or completely chicken I decided chicken was expendable in my life. As I learned about food concerns, I phased out or abruptly stopped eating those things.

I took positions with soy, wheat, agave nectar, syrup that was not 100% maple, and microwave ovens. I had my successes and challenges with respect to complying with my eating standards. When I succeeded, I was proud of myself and celebrated my discipline, which fed my SSW. If I bragged about it I was seeking attention and recognition from others, which would have represented PSW. So they can co-exist.

I teach a workshop, which is also the name of one of my forthcoming books, "Being Better by Eating Better". Though I am always being asked if I am writing a cookbook, I always explain how people can get recipes from virtually anywhere so that is not my focus. The most difficult thing for people is looking at how and why they eat what they do. I have been a vegan or a vegetarian for the past 23 years. In the book, one of the things I discuss is examining what things hinder you from eating better.

One of those things that create a potential hindrance to the eating process I identified as 'peer-pressure'. This is what happens when you are on a 'no added fat' eating regimen, for example, and your friends or family eat whatever they desire. You are almost guaranteed to have more than one person attempt to sway you from your eating specification and eat what they want to eat. They will say things like, "you only live once", "we do not get to do this together often" or "you have been doing really well so just indulge this once".

This can be for any restriction you have made and it still will not matter, there is going to be an attempt to assassinate your agenda. You might decide to stop drinking alcohol, smoking (whatever), eating red meat, eating high fructose corn syrup, eating heavily past 7pm, eating and drinking simultaneously, eating fried foods or eating when you are not hungry. In every case, someone will offer a reason why you should not, even though all of those things are to your benefit maximizing overall health.

This is not just peer-pressure but it is also an opportunity to add PSW points. The thought process is, I was strong and influential enough to get you to come off of your regimen and do what I wanted and willed for you. We always feel good when we have power or pseudo power over someone else. We feel good when people listen to us and take our advice. That adds worth indeed. I would love for you all to take heed to my reasoning and sell 10 million copies of this book but I can only trust that you will see the value in assessing the source and intention of your self-worth building efforts.

Granted, I have not had this happen to me for a while now. I think people are clear that, as a vegan chef, it is useless to try to convince me to downgrade when I am constantly looking to improve my selections and eat better and better. In my, Being Better by Eating Better workshop everyone can usually relate to this phenomenon. One way you know that this is pseudo is if you find yourself telling someone else, "yea, I had to tell her to go on ahead and eat that, it will not kill you". If you are bragging or celebrating your achievements regarding someone else's actions or inactions, beware of PSW.

I am proud to say I do not judge folks though people are always assuming I would as a vegan. They constantly apologize if they are having a conversation about some non-vegan item that they love, while in front of me. There is always someone who eats better than I do so I am not interested in judging another. I have been on my path and I respect that they are on theirs.

I have worked in the natural foods industry all of my adult life so my transition was relatively easier. My adult career began at Sevananda Natural Foods Cooperative in Little Five Points, Atlanta, GA, back in March of 1991. It is interesting how I came to work there. My girlfriend, at the time, was the first person I knew who walked around with nuts and berries in her bag, who was not my Aunt and Uncle from

Brownsville whom I referenced in previous chapters. They were the trendsetters of the family for eating better while growing up. She knew I was looking for a job and sent me there. I was feeling really good about myself because I dropped my app off on a Sunday and got an interview the next day which was also my hire date. I was glad that they were impressed with my person and minimal retail background.

The sister would break up with me three weeks later while at my birthday party, in my walk-in closet. She then went back downstairs and danced with my dudes like nothing happened. Yep, I remember it like it was yesterday because, from a PSW perspective, I took it personally and felt hurt that I was not wanted anymore by her. I sat in my closet for hours after that and listened to slow jams and just sang and cried. She is responsible for setting me on this path. Her role in my life was served.

I can say, from a SSW perspective, if you are not attracted to me, I get it. Aside from some practical things I need to improve upon in general, I cannot feel bad if I am not deemed an attractive mate. I can be smart, relatively good looking, smell nice, dance well, prepare food well and offer an uplifting energy but still be an unattractive mate, so I will still walk away feeling good about who I have come to be. My SSW is and will be intact. That is because I understand the importance of purpose, mine, and others. We meet people for specific reasons and purposes. It is not going to be just about who smiles at you or wants to go to the movies with you.

When people tell me they tried to go whole foods plant-based for 2-weeks but could not do it, I completely understand. It is like dating someone but breaking up with them sooner rather than later. You have to respect the process of eating the same way you have to respect the process of dating. Get to know your new eating style and how you can enjoy it the same way you have to converse with this new person long before getting physical. Feel great before making the switch allowing your SSW to lead you, instead of trying to prove a point to everyone around you about what you have chosen before actually being ready for it. I can meet a gorgeous woman and tell everyone how great we are going to be but I have not courted her yet. Until then, I am just bringing attention to myself, which is PSW based.

So I am at Sevananda learning a plethora of ways to eat without eating meat and dairy. This is not too long after I expressed my inability to see no meat in my life. I was full of new knowledge and insisted on spreading the word to everyone I reached, convincing them to leave the meat alone. I became the food police. Employees would congregate in the break room to eat and I would actually go around the table assessing who was eating what.

I realize now how irritating that must have been. Even though I did it in a joking manner, I sincerely cared about what they were eating. I still nullified my intentions with my need to satisfy my PSW. I felt like it was my obligation to teach everyone what I now knew. I felt more valuable to everyone because I had information. I finally stopped policing the area, thankfully before I pissed someone off enough to tell me about myself. I realized how irritating that was when it was being done to me, which is usually how we realize the effect we have on others.

I still ate all of the favorite meat substitutes and drank all of the dairy alternatives, so that included tofu, soy milk, wheat gluten and texturized vegetable protein. I, in turn, had more informed folks coming to me with information I did not necessarily want to hear while I was hooking up this great tasting ground soy dish sautéed with vegetables. Part of it was I did not want to believe that these things were as bad as I was being led to believe. I just mentioned to a dear friend that I refrain from random lectures on eating better when I am out and about. I am, however, adamant about not drinking soda. I will express how detrimental soda is in the sugar addiction realm. I also respect that it is not easy to break this habit/addiction just as it is for smoking, drinking alcohol or eating bread.

Have you come in contact with someone who brags about eating a pound of meat at the steakhouse? How about the vegan who had a big salad that filled them up nicely but did not weigh them down? Have you had someone brag about how much food they ate in one sitting? How about around Thanksgiving? Bragging is a relative of PSW and should raise a flag.

There is another component to this subject matter which is reflective of the name of this chapter. Seeing as we all have values and standards it would seem that, arguably, the number one or two life-sustaining actions we can take is the consumption of food and drink. I would say that it is only second to the mental/spiritual component of being well.

You have heard the analogy before about how we treat our car better than our body. I recognize the truth in that while also seeing how we do more to the outside of the car than the internal workings. It can be easily explained by way of the PSW perspective since we do the same with our body.

The car has to be seen. The car is also a significant part of the PSW image. The rims, the tinted windows, the tires, the vanity license plates all play a role in presenting who we are by way of that vehicle. For optimal performance with our vehicles, we could focus on any of the following: the gas brand and octane, oil brand and type, (high mileage, synthetic, etc.), transmission fluid, gas treatment, antifreeze and windshield wiper fluid, etc. We might spend thousands on rims for the car to look good but get the cheapest antifreeze from the store. We may pay several hundreds or thousands of dollars for a stereo, as an upgrade to an already decent audio sound system. We get lights underneath the car and behind the wheels. We get high-performance tires spending over $200 easily per tire. The car looks great! We also got the fancy LED headlights and upgraded our headlight lenses. We added the chrome pipe for the exhaust for sound effect and for looks. If the car broke down tomorrow, none of the accessories would help to make the care run again.

  The car would run better and longer if we use the best fluids for the car. Obviously, the same goes for the body. The outside of the body is mostly about muscles, clear skin, hair, and hue. For some, this list could include eyelashes and make-up. In the spirit of the analogy, I am leaving out clothing. We have nail appointments every Friday, where we sit in front of the mostly Asian woman with the mask on to block the toxins from them.

  We get our haircuts, hair coloring, and hair styling regularly. We even get perms to straighten our hair still, even though the ingredients are linked to cancer. We spend Saturday afternoons at the local Ulta because make-up is still a big part of our presentation. We spend money on skincare from the department store, drug store, beauty supply store and TV infomercials. We exercise, exhibiting tremendous discipline and inner strength for hours every week. Why is it so difficult to spend money on groceries instead of the dollar menu?

Food provides nutrients to sustain, cure, improve and heal. You can eat your way to less fat, clearer skin, stronger hair. You do not have to be a vegan to achieve this, but you do have to accept responsibility for what you feed your children and your selves. I am talking to me as well. As a vegan, I am not absent from tendencies that do not serve me in the best way every day. You do have to come face to face with your addictions and realize, you may not be able to see yourself not eating meat because of the chemicals in the meat to keep you addicted to it. You can research this to find the truth in it.

There are things that have no business in our bodies. We seem to use our ego conveniently. "He better not come to me with that BS". "I hope she does not think she is getting in my car acting like that!". "Y'all are going to get out my house if you think you are going to play and tear up my furniture?" The government and the dairy industry told you that 'milk does the body good'. They told you that it provides your most efficient source of calcium. They told you that it prevents arthritis. You refuse to refute these even though there are plenty of physicians who were willing to finally speak out against these claims. There must be something to this because doctors are turning up dead because of their whistle-blowing activities. Remember that PSW does not like to be wrong. Being wrong takes away from our worth when you operate out of your pseudo self. We do not wish to accept that what we are putting into our bodies is toxic. Well, what about those of us who know the truth, but cannot muster up enough discipline to consume an alternative?

The people who make round-up take the same chemicals that kill weeds and pest and they genetically implant that chemical into the food (seed) and then grow it without worrying about the need to spray it. They say that they have tested it and that it is safe. They seem to have not tested it for long-term effects, nor have they allowed the test results to be reviewed by the potential consumers of those same products.

As a matter of fact, they do not even want you to know that they have genetically modified those products. That is why labeling acts requiring the disclosure of GMO ingredients continue to be shot down vote after vote, state after state.

Yet, we will continue to consume these products like corn, wheat, soy, potatoes, grapes, and berries with no regard for its GMO status. The chemical that kills a tiny bug cannot possibly harm big ole me, can it? It is also linked to cancers, which most of us have been affected by with friends and loved ones. There are great and grand reasons for genetically modifying foods. When there are deception and secrets involved in the process, I am inclined to speak out against it.

It may not matter to you that these same companies have entered the vaccination industry, which has linked, at least suspected, of contributing to the unimaginable growth in Autism and Asperger's Syndrome. You will still get two and three vaccinations in one visit even while, potentially cancer-causing, formaldehyde is one of the ingredients.

Is horse meat worthy to be in your body? Should you take the stress of an animal about to get slaughtered? Is it wise to eat animals that have been kept healthy by receiving antibiotics such that they will no longer work when you need to fight an infection? Does soy really take 8 hours to digest in the body? Is bottled water in plastic cancer-causing bottles? Is bottled water acidic and leaving us vulnerable to more degenerative diseases? Is higher PH water still no good if it is in a non-BPA bottle? Are aluminum pots and pans detrimental to one's health and wellness? Is a bowel movement every other day okay if my doctor says so? Does caffeine stunt the growth of children? Is Folic Acid the same as Folate? Is one better than the other? Is it fine to eat a fruit salad with watermelon, grapes, oranges, pomegranate seeds and cantaloupe? Does my self-worth play a role in my choices to eat things I know are not good for me, just because I might feel bad about myself?

    I do not have all of the answers. My way of eating is not the best way. But, there is no reason why you cannot research these claims I am making, except you do not want to be wrong about the stances you have taken or, I am sorry, you just do not have the time. I did not mention this in the previous chapter, but we are often so locked into our PSW that we refuse to consider that any other religion or spiritual ideology could be more effective for us than our current one because that would require that we acknowledge that we were not doing the best thing for us. I recall how difficult it was to leave the WWCG especially since I was so invested that I was essentially recruiting people myself.

    I know of people who refuse to taste my food because, if it is good tasting they will have no excuse for doing better. PSW must be examined to determine how much it dictates your actions or in-actions.

Moving Forward

Eating and drinking are two important opportunities to feel great about ourselves. Every meal is an opportunity to eat better. My objective is to have you consider what you are putting inside of yourself and ask if it is worthy to be in your body, which is a question rarely asked or acted upon. With so many health concerns we experience one would think it would be easy to leave soda alone. Soda, the same thing I need to buy today so that I can clean the corrosion off of my car battery, is what people drink daily.

I just want folks to take as many opportunities as possible to celebrate themselves and move in their purpose, not to be distracted by how many prescription medicines they need to take. Honesty with self will be the first step toward us moving past our weaknesses and distractions. I want us to see our reflection in each other and not judge each other for our weaknesses in eating and drinking. I want us to operate out of our own eating standards and not be coerced by someone else to drop your standard and go lower as opposed to better.

Chapter 10

PSW Means I Get Some, SSW Means I Gives it Up

    I saved this chapter for last because it is the most critical and possesses the most frequent occurrences of exhibiting PSW. The name of this chapter is a spin-off of another one of my upcoming books, "Boys Get Some, Men Give it Up". I realized while writing this book that the two terms are practically interchangeable. You will see what I am talking about by the time you complete this chapter.
    There are two key things that move and motivate people in the world, as I see it, Money and Sex. Money is an absolute need to live, on the most basic and fundamental level, unless your resources or bartering leverage satisfies those same basic needs. Practically every resource requires the exchange of money. Sex is almost as absolute for the sake of continuing humanity. If Sex were not delightfully feeling it would be considered a chore and would not the focal point of the lives of most of us. We live in a time where humanity could be continued through the use of science. The semen of a man can simply be inserted into the uterus of a woman upon

ovulation and with a successful penetration by the sperm cell, the egg is fertilized.

Nonetheless, since sex is highly recreational, and it feels great both physically as well as mentally, it makes my list because it seems to be the best form of pleasure. It also draws in money like it has never before in history. These two are also responsible for the bulk of how people choose to carry out their pseudo self-worth building. This final chapter will focus on sex and its intimate relation with PSW.

There is much to discuss on this subject that expands the Pseudo Self-Worth conversation. We will look at meaningless, empty, pseudo Self-Worth building sex and the building up of the relationship that sometimes accompanies the reckless and premature sexual exchange.

The cars, the house, the clothes, the jewelry, the titles, and the dropping of knowledge all contribute to that leverage used to reel that brother or sister into getting to know you better, or well enough to like you. When people like us we feel valuable and sometimes, we will do whatever we can to be liked.

Men are usually the aggressors but women are also quite clever and creative when they have interest in a dude. I hear a lot of brothers tell me their stories of these assertive women, but I do not have any firsthand knowledge of what they talk about. Women spend a lot of time and energy to do whatever needs to get done to be attractive to men. As a man, I recognize that we are on a different scale than women because we pay for sex or put out money for sex disproportionately from a woman, seemingly. Paying for sex includes, buying drinks, meals, paying bills, as well as engaging in actual prostitution. In short, we do a lot to gain access to women sexually. Unfortunately, what this also translates into is inappropriate actions by way of harassment and assault on women, by men.

The beginning stage of 'getting some' for a man is what I experienced one day which was a thought, 'what if I got a smile from every young lady I glanced at while in my daily travels. My pseudo self would love that so much. Just a quick note: I grew up in an era where a female would walk past and the male would say, "yo what's up shorty", even if she was not short. Today, the words might be more along the lines of 'Whattup Ma? Can I get that math or dm you on the gram?' I remember what would happen if the female did not comply or cooperate with the approach, 'F—k you B---ch!'

I used to focus on the ego when discussing this reaction but I have shifted the explanation to reflect the PSW factor as well. That response by sisters told us, the aggressors, we were not worthy of their attention and energy. This was a major blow to the self-worth, which is why the reaction was retaliatory. The retaliation is because she took his worth away in that instance so he is going to attempt to take hers as well.

Now, let's expand this thought to consider every woman I was attracted to, responding affirmatively to my sexual advances. That would mean whatever I was wearing, driving, or whatever game I was spitting was working. If everybody I wanted to like me, liked me, that would be amazing. The best or the worst part would be, they would not even know the real me. I would not have to work on anything toward self-improvement. When these women started with the drama I would just cut them loose and check for the next one. My pseudo self-worth is not based on them knowing me, but on them accepting and being attracted to me based on what *they* like or value.

While in PSW mode, I am not interested in sex with the same woman more than once or maybe just a couple of times, because of a couple of reasons. The first and primary reason is, she has already fed my PSW so I no longer have an appetite for her. I had to put in whatever work was necessary to draw her in so now that I have reached the objective, the thrill has left. Since I can never be too full of PSW I must push on to the next one for more value-added experiences. I have nothing to prove anymore because my game worked. I enticed you so much with my PSW inspired self that you were willing to disregard and dishonor your universal portal, your Vagina, and Uterus. (See Ma'at em Maakheru for her books on the magnificence of the womb, "UnWombded: Unlocking the Universal Uterus".)

Unfortunately, for you women, because there are so many other beautiful women out there I, as a man, will look out for and be open to the next woman to add to my worth. That is the reason why I will ignore your follow-up calls, texts, emails and messages on social media.

Let me say this very clearly, there will always be a sister that we find just as gorgeous if not more so than you. I used to wonder how brothers could cheat on the likes of Halle Berry, Beyonce, Chili, and Hillary Clinton, (just playing on that last one). What I am now clear on is drama and attitude trump beauty on any day. Even in the absence of drama, if another gorgeous woman is checking for you and you need that value added to your PSW account, you will welcome the attention and opportunity. This will be the case even it means violating your relationship or marriage. I do not know what your man's motivations are outside of his PSW account needing to be replenished. I do know that this is one of the key reasons why men and women cheat.

When I was single I had a hard time having sex with a woman if I could not see a bright future between us, for whatever reason. I talked about the 'butt naked games' I used to play back in the day. Although I slept with, took showers with and messed around with sisters in those days, I respected the energy exchange enough to know not to penetrate that vortex. I was happy that they wanted to take showers with me. I knew or thought that for a woman to allow me to see her naked, I must have been special. I was clear about my limits with everyone I did that with. Even so, some actually thought they could shift me off my path and intention. In that respect, I set a standard for myself and stuck with it even though they 'wanted me'. It is not always about someone wanting you as it could have been the idea of you. It could just be that you are relatively *safe* to have intercourse versus others who may want or need more energy.

I know that my resistance to having sexual intercourse made these women more attracted to me. I suspect that it was more about the circumstance and situation than it was about me. My PSW would say otherwise. Their PSW was at play at that point because they were convinced that there was something 'wrong' with them because it did not make sense that I would not take advantage of what every other man had, their willingness to give their physical bodies an energy up.

To be clear about the time frame, this was at any time after 1994. I do not want anyone boycotting book signings calling me SSW fake. "He did not seem to have any issues trying the hit the high score with me". The only women I have had intercourse with since then was my ex-wife and my current wife, which I am proud to say. Here is the thing I knew: once I released what followed was the 'uh oh moment'. That is when reality hits and you realize, what you have done.

This PSW topic gets even more interesting when you break down the sex piece. I shared this in a Facebook post back in the spring of 2017 which some thought was a bit too visual. A vagina is a warm and moist place most of the time. The penis loves this environment and it could be in that place joyfully without regard for who is hosting the vagina. What I am saying is at the end of the day it really does not matter who you are for a pseudo self-worther. I can close my eyes and make the experience with whomever I want it to be with. Simultaneously, it really feeds and replenishes PSW when you are categorized as pretty, fly, dope, gorgeous, beautiful, cute, butter or a dime. When we find you attractive and we will get confirmation from friends, family, and others, that will helps when we brag about 'tapping that'.

This is also a good time to address erections and the potential causes. Yes, seeing your naked body, because it is 'A' naked body, might offer an erection. Having to urinate intensely may trigger this response too. Rubbing up on you in the club while listening to Bob Marley, Gregory Isaacs or Dub Addis might do it as well. Dreaming about rocks might give us an erection. As Eddie Murphy joked about, the wind blowing might give us an erection. My point is having an erection does not really have anything to do with you, so please do not make that a self-worth opportunity women. You should not get too happy you got us to that erectile state nor should you be saddened that you could not. We are so conditioned to respond to touch, sight and thought that, again, we are just going through the motions.

When men are 'getting some' they are taking the opportunity to receive what you are offering. The energy of the word sound is, 'I am getting some ass', not 'I am getting some affectionate energy from', your name here,_____. There is no attention given to you the person, the soul, just your genitalia. So, ladies, when your mindset is 'I am giving him some', he will gladly 'get it'. At that point, you have given him a depository for his ejaculation that could just as easily have gone elsewhere. Your naked body is simply 'a naked body' before it is 'your naked body'.

Let me be more specific. Everybody likes a nice looking butt that protrudes out from the lower back. It is celebrated and glorified by men and woman. We have decided that it is nice to hold onto, press up against and caress when appropriate. If the host of a not-so-well-endowed butt is a visually and spiritually beautiful woman, we would only deny a relationship if PSW were our dominant source of worth. If PSW is our major motivation, you do not want to be with us, I promise. Otherwise, we will caress your flat butt or your humongous extra large panties size butt and still get just as aroused and erect as if you were 'holding' like the woman on an Outkast CD cover.

The same goes for breast, and this is very important to present also, because of stress women have when needing to have a mastectomy due to breast cancer or when other health matters that warrant the procedure. PSW based motivations force men to want women that every other man will envy because of how great she looks. We break up with a beautiful woman our goal is to get a 'better-looking' woman, not necessarily a better woman. This is what PSW does to us.

Another part of this conversation is, we are always looking to tell dudes about our experiences with other women. This is often because our PSW loves to be celebrated for our achievements and having sex with a female we just met is worthy of celebration. Sometimes we tell each other about a beautiful woman we see while out and about. That is not necessarily about PSW because we are celebrating what we saw, not what we engaged in. Married dudes having sex with their wives might make a comment about their energy exchange, pending or just recently occurring, because of the frequency of sexual relations in marriage drops so drastically for so many dudes. I do not deem that a PSW moment, we are just happy and want to share our joy.

If I am a male operating out of Pseudo self-worth I am not going to be satisfied with one sexual partner. The challenge and celebration that comes with many women being interested in giving of themselves sexually make us feel worthy. Once we have you the challenge shifts to maybe keeping 'you', while also keeping 'her' or 'them', depending on how strong our game is or how resilient our PSW is. This is not the recipe that all brothers, who creep, operate from but if they looked at it, I am sure they would see their PSW reflection based on the behavior exhibited.

You might be a victim of PSW, but not be so inclined to cheat. You may just want or enjoy the attention. Case in point, I went to the 28th annual Malcolm X Festival at the historic West End Park, in Atlanta, GA. I wanted to wear my 'I ♥ Black Woman' shirt to the festival that could easily be named the 'beautiful black woman festival'. I got the shirt from my beautiful sisters at Knotti By Nature Natural Hair Salon, in Louisburg, NC while at the Harambee Community Fest and immediately thought about where I could wear it.

I did not wear it to the festival because I felt like it was going to draw attention to me, more so than celebrate my regard for melanin dominant women. Would I have loved the attention, even as a married man? Absolutely! Was it going to be rooted in PSW? Absolutely! I wanted the attention but I could not be in the middle of writing this book and do something that blatant. I had a vision that I would walk into the park and women would just roll up and hug me on the strength of my endorsement for them. In my PSW dreams…, which I do have.

My Queens, sisters, ladies and homegirls, you are not forgotten in this process. Here are some things for you all to reflect upon. We, males, experience the scenario where you are not interested in us until it boosts your PSW to steal or distract us from our partner, girl, boo, wife or whatever term we use to classify our committed relationship. It is one thing to get a guy to want to place his penis inside of you, but it must mean that your vagina is platinum if he is willing to place his penis inside of you even though he already has someone he can be with sexually. Now, this is PSW living! This is something you might say without actually saying it.

When you go to the club, the Greek Fest or the driving strip, where you know dudes will be in full effect, your process of getting dressed is often times focused on what will make you stand out in the crowd. The question becomes, how many dudes will you want to holler at you or, even better, will want to spend money and time with you instead of the next female? 'I do not want to be felt on but I do want dudes to see my butt in its fullness so I will put on these thongs to really allow them to focus on my cheeks'. 'My breast need to be perky and exposed enough for dudes to visualize what they look like but not enough to see my nipple because that would not be appropriate'. 'I need to have maximum cleavage and, since it's my body, I can do what I want to'. 'I want to be sexually appealing but I do not want them to think of me only as a sex object'.

When I knew a sister was striving and starving for attention, I gave her none, as much as I really wanted to look. I did this for two reasons:

I knew I could and would see another appealing body in due time, and I did not want to encourage that behavior. The PSW driven behavior that, in my estimation, took things too far with how much was being revealed, is what I am referring to. With that said, I had to work hard to look her in her eyes when talking and not 'down there'. Sometimes it is unfair because you may not be interested in her breast but you are drawn to what is written on her shirt. Dudes, you have to keep your eyes at eye level! I know it takes a lot of discipline, but you will feel great about yourself upon completing the task. At Least I do.

    The same way men sometimes see a woman as another host of an arousing anatomy, woman have proven that they are sometimes interested in just having a penis inside of them from a relatively nice or safe guy. They may not be attached to the person, just the product, and a likely host. This would be another good time to reflect on "Whatz In Your Womb". You have brothers walking around thinking they got it going on and really they were at the 'right' place at the 'right' time.

    I am here to tell you ladies, you are beautiful in your long sundress that is loose fitting and flowing. You are beautiful slim or chunky. You are attractive when you wear a head wrap or you are rocking afro puffs. You are attractive 100 pounds overweight or 50 pounds underweight. When your beauty, which is not your shell, vessel or body, oozes and exudes from you, spirit emanating and blaring, self-worth sincere, stable and viable, you will draw the desired and complementary energy to you accordingly.

You will have men eager to give it up to you also. Why? Women (Wombmen) are great beings! We all come from women, which is divine in itself. We were all women at conception before some of us shifted to the male form. Our genitalia, as men, are underdeveloped versions of the female genitalia. Before we even get to address a woman we need to be in a state of celebration for women.

I am more than a male, a boy, a sexual organ, a sperm donor and a builder of PSW. I am a Man. I have learned about my spirit, my energy, my purpose and my power sources. I chose not to just ejaculate wherever and with whoever I wish to. I chose not to succumb to who my hormones deem worthy of me. I have a life force inside of me and when I release my semen into the world I am wasting life force and energy, often times with someone I do not deem worthy to receive this energy. Maybe that is why I get stalked or get my car keyed when I do not give them the attention they needed after we engaged in true grown folk business, sex.

As aforementioned, I went through a period in my 20's where I decided I created enough drama for myself having irresponsible sexual intercourse and creating an emotional connection with females who I was not mentally and spiritually connected to beforehand. Not only did I have sex with these females, I really tried to make it a memorable experience for them. From a self-worth perspective, I wanted them to enjoy what I was serving. From an ego perspective, I wanted the talk around the water cooler to be that I had it going on.

Quick note, women do not have to scream and lose feeling in their leg for the exchange to be enjoyable. I have learned that woman can be quiet and still and in a state of euphoria while enjoying the exchange. I thought I was not being appreciated, but we discussed it and I was informed accordingly. PSW keeps us from wanting to have the conversation because we do not want to hear anything but, "you were great!" When I began to honor my energy and spirit that is when I stopped having sex with anyone willing and deemed pretty enough to tell about. If I were not able to see sharing parental responsibilities and/or seeing us as life partners and would not and did not engage.

My SSW blossomed as I was able to walk away from naked woman unscathed but also leaving them uplifted and enlightened, to whatever extent they felt that. I never got confirmation from any of the sisters I declined sexual energy from but my SSW knew that I left them in a better place even if emotionally they had to adjust at first. I did not necessarily need to receive feedback, recognition or celebration from any of them.

This is what 'giving it up' looks like for and from me. I have deemed you worthy to offer my energy to merge with yours. There will be a conversation about what works for you and what does not. This will include viable positions, sensitive areas, and an open invitation to offer feedback and direction throughout the exchange. (What worked for your past partners may not necessarily work for the present one.) I am looking forward to adding joy to your being. I am looking forward to spending an unlimited amount of time doing so. There will be a lot of touching, caressing, kissing and caring for you. I am deciding at the outset whether I will release while engaging in this energy exchange with you.

I am giving you an experience because you are regarded as a great person in my life and you deserve this. I feel great about sharing with you and look forward to holding you after we have shared. I already know, from our conversation, that you are not verbally expressive so I do not have to go in harder or deeper to get you to scream to feel secure that you are enjoying it.

This is not a porno film and my self-worth is not dependent on the bed breaking, the ceiling collapsing or the cops knocking. If and when I release, there will not be an 'uh-oh' factor unless it was remembering that I did not take the live cheesecake out of the freezer before we began.

There is so much drama associated with sex and sexual energy exchanges. This book is offering an opportunity to re-evaluate what we do and why, and determining whether it is serving our deepest and highest self best. It is my will that our behaviors around sex and all of its subsidiaries, how we use sexuality for attention, come from a sincere place and not a needy, false, misleading place. We are not our bodies, we just operate out of them.

Love Being A Part is a relationship program and service my wife and I facilitate. One point that comes out of this program is the idea of finding and living your purpose and then enjoying the opportunity to share it with a partner. The alternative is to not know your purpose and find someone, who then becomes a major part of your new found purpose. This scenario offers vulnerability once the person chooses another or you lose interest in the person. With the relationship, also goes your purpose for living and being. With no purpose, to focus on and celebrate, there is a greater probability of a PSW driven life

Moving Forward

Take care of your body because it is the right thing to do if you are striving to maximize your quality of life. If people notice your muscles and shape, buttocks and pecks in the process, so be it. Know that your spirit is your most important asset, not your ass. Get closer to being comfortable with the potential co-parent of your child(ren) by regarding who you are as well as who your partner(s) is/are. Ladies, just because 'Craig and nem' want to have sex with you does not mean that you are special to them. You are special, but you need not seek confirmation from someone who has a phallus who is appreciative of any warm, moist box to place it in. Men, if you are living above your means for the sake of attracting sexual partners, continue to do you! Know that it is neither serving you nor will you appreciate it when your daughter is one of those superficial women easily influenced by a drink, a nice car and some empty compliments.

Check out the likes of Dr. Llaila Afrika, Dr. Consir Thot, Dr. Kaba Haiwatha Kamene, Baba

Wanique Khemi Tehuti Shabazz, Dr. Patricia Crisp and many others for clarity on information and perspectives presented in this chapter.

Chapter 11

Moving Forward Most Progressively

There is no doubt in my mind that this self-worth philosophy can change the world we live in. So much of whom we identify ourselves with and how we carry ourselves is tied to our self-worth. As you move forward, make this new concept of identifying and calculating self-worth a big part in your daily movements.

Emotions and emotional reactions play a major role in assessing the weight and source of your self-worth. Try this exercise: Take an hour out of your daily routine and monitor your various emotional sensations and what you did once in that state of reacting or responding to it. If you are in a position to journal during this hour session, please do so. You can do this while playing with the children, watching a movie or TV program, during a meeting at work, while driving, or taking a walk with your 'lovely one'.

Let me offer an example that inspired this exercise. I was pulling into Trader Joes in Chapel Hill, NC, which I shop at especially because of prices and stated food quality standards. Their standards include no artificial colors, flavors, preservatives and sweeteners and no genetically modified organisms. From a SSW perspective, it feels good to go in there, as a regular customer, and get plenty of pleasant greetings and energy from the staff every time. It may be because I greet everyone and they reciprocate it by sharing their good energy in their greeting.

Continuing with the story, as I am pulling in, rear end first, there is a car pulling out, rear end first. I pull forward in preparation to back in, but two pedestrians walk behind my car as they are heading toward the store. I wait for them to pass, recognizing that the other car has to wait for me before he can go forward unless he decides he is going to attempt to pass behind me. It seems like he considered that for a minute, which disturbed me. I felt or created a displeased emotion surface from him. As I began to pull back, he changed his direction a bit to go in front of me. He seemed to be disturbed, based on my assessment of his facial expression. I also thought so because of what I imagined he might be thinking about. I would have been thinking the same thing I suspected he was, if I were in his position and had to wait when I did not want to.

As he drove past, I telepathically talked him down off of his emotional position by explaining to him, calmly, how ridiculous it was for him to be upset by that situation. I 'stepped to the side of my emotion' and observed how I felt and how I moved through it. I did not even need to get upset by the situation, but I was. I was not upset or reactionary enough to address him, curse him, yell, shout, beef, or offer emotionally charged hand gestures, but I did complain by talking him 'off the ledge'. I was really talking to and dealing with me. Even though I felt great about my SSW, I recognized that the suggestion by the other driver that my decision-making in that parking lot was poor was actually a threat to my self-worth. My PSW took over and engaged that driver telepathically. Do you understand how subtle this can be sometimes?

Anytime our self-worth is 'under attack' our emotions are triggered. We tie ourselves to how we express ourselves emotionally, no matter what the emotional state is. For instance, I feel great when I am in a great mood or state of being. I greet people more readily and minimize self-inflicted distractions about what people are thinking about me. Examine, log and get better about remaining in a 'most progressive' state of building. Allow this exercise to serve you on this journey of uplifting SSW and pressing down PSW.

Here is another exercise for you to consider in this process: address the judgment factor. Judgment is a major player in the determination of our self-worth and emotional state. There is a connotation associated with 'being judged' that is not favorable. There are scriptures that address judgment to support the understood energy that accompanies judgment. I would like to consider, of the many definitions of judgment, the definition that offers 'opinion' as a synonym instead.

Your opinion or assessment of a given topic or situation, or more importantly, the opinion or assessment someone has or expresses about you, offers another opportunity to identify and measure SSW as well as the tendency to resort to PSW.

The exercise is, take stock of as many opinions (judgments) you have processed about whatever or whomever in the course of your daily movements. Then itemize how many of these opinions were critical versus favorable. After this assessment, identify the source of your position prompting the position taken on the various matters judged.

This exercise serves you in a number of ways. The first thing it will do is assess for you how often you take a position on life matters and whether you have tendencies that are balanced or imbalanced. Are you more or less complimentary about your assessments? Why do you hold that opinion on a given subject or situation? This too will provide great information for moving forward most progressively. When you are in the role of judging, assessing or offering an opinion about someone or something else, not you, it offers a perspective that makes it easier to receive judgments, assessments, and opinions from others. It is vital to go through this process especially because we judge based on what we think about ourselves often. If your self-worth is compromised, you will give no one else credit for valuing you either, causing you to consider actions likened to what I started this book with, committing suicide.

The folks who do not go that route are still more prone to move out of a place of PSW. If you are reading this book, you now know you do not have to take your life. You also do not need to take the life of someone else. You do have to identify, focus on and celebrate the Sincere Self-Worth that resides in you. It feels better and better the more you unearth about yourself. You are worthy to be in your presence.

I know many people who have 'judgment issues' where they judge harshly and often or they are constantly processing how people are assessing them in an unfavorable manner. Because self-worth is directly influenced by judgment, this will bring everything that contributes to our worth right to the surface. This exercise will serve you well, especially if you effectively apply, honesty, and awareness.

Please pay attention to you. Look in the mirror and talk to yourself about what you are doing that is better than before. Talk about how you can and will do even better. The two most important things you can represent are honesty and awareness, which begins with the self. Please see your reflection of self and self-worth in others by paying attention to those around you.

I know folks who, for the sake of their unstable self-worth, have to tell you all about whatever they know. You might have a conversation but there is no actual exchange. You might actually get to contribute to the conversation, but they are the authors of the conversation allowing you to participate only in a passive manner. Even if you do attempt to say something worthwhile, it may not matter because what you say does not matter to someone striving for PSW. They will stay the course and continue to talk about what they know. You do not have to be that person, and if that is you, you do not have to be that person anymore. Please deal with the PSW motivation behind this so that people can receive you more sincerely and lovingly. These are usually the people I irritate myself the most with being around. (They do not irritate me unless I allow it, so I irritate myself.)

Remember that PSW is fulfilling but not as sustained as SSW. It feels great to catch yourself in PSW mode and shift over to SSW. Lives can and will be changed as we put focus, not on the ego, but on self-worth, yours. If you are that supposed leader or you want to be the leader because of the prestige, know that the people closest to you regard you the least, but the clueless people may cheer you and carry you through the streets. They will do this up until the point they realize how little regard you have for them. You can dress as elegantly as you wish and wear the most beautiful geles, but you have to disrobe at some point and when that time comes you might want to actually check yourself. Maybe you are fine as long as people do not tell you that they tolerate you instead of enjoy you.

None of us really like being told about our opportunities for improvement even when we value the feedback and respect how it will help us in our profession, journey or experience. I did not want to hear that I rubbing too hard while giving that amateur massage but I know what to do for the next time to bring about more joy and comfort. We would like to get it right the first time. There is a difference between thinking something and knowing it. Know that you are worthy and do not base your worth on how many people tell you so. Simultaneously, align yourself with folks who are more likely to recognize your greatness instead of rolling with 'haters'. These are folks who see you shining but disregard or disparage your achievements because it outshines theirs.

Pseudo self-worth is tempting and opportunities are plentiful. Make your self-worth strong and sincere, through honesty and awareness. Change your world, your community, your household and yourself by consistently asking yourself that very question I ask in the title of this book, Is Your Self-Worth Pseudo or Sincere?

Made in the USA
Columbia, SC
24 April 2018